FINANCIAL RISK MANAGEMENT

UNIT 7

RISK ASSESSMENT AND INTEREST RATE RISK

Financial Strategy

Prepared for the Course Team by Richard Wheatcroft
with contributions by Clare Minchington
and Bernardo Bátiz-Lazo

The Open University
BUSINESS
SCHOOL

OPEN UNIVERSITY COURSE TEAM

Core Group

Professor Janette Rutterford, *Production and Presentation Course Team Co-Chair and Author*

David Barnes, *Author*

Bernardo Bátiz-Lazo, *Presentation Course Team Co-Chair and Author*

Marcus Davison, *Author*

Keith Dixon, *Author*

Graham Francis, *Author*

Carmel de Nahlik

Jan Gadella, *Author*

Margaret Greenwood

Heinz Kassier

Tony Anthoni, *Course Manager*

Clare Minchington, *Author*

Kathy Reay, *Course Team Assistant*

Pat Sucher, *Author*

Patricia Swannell, *Author*

Richard Wheatcroft, *Author*

External Assessor

Professor Paul Draper, Walter Scott and Partners Professor of Finance, University of Edinburgh

Production Team

Sylvan Bentley, *Picture Researcher*

John Bradley, *Design Group Co-ordinator*

Martin Brazier, *Graphic Designer*

Henry Dougherty, *Editor*

Jenny Edwards, *Product Quality Assistant*

Anne Faulkner, *Information Specialist*

John Garne, *Computing Consultant*

Roy Lawrance, *Graphic Artist*

David Libbert, *BBC Series Producer*

Richard Mole, *Director of Production OUBS*

Kathy Reay, *Course Team Assistant*

Linda K. Smith, *Project Controller*

Doreen Tucker, *Compositor*

Steve Wilkinson, *BBC Series Producer*

External Critical Readers

Stephen Abbott

George Buckberry

Linda Cinderey

Roland Davis

Angela Garrett

Jane Hughes

Ed Hutt

Rosemary F Johnson

Geoff Jones

Robin Joy

David Kirk

Archie McArthur

Richard Mischak

Professor Chris Napier

Eugene Power

Manvinder Singh

Tony Whitford

The Open University, Walton Hall, Milton Keynes MK7 6AA

First published 1998. Second edition 1999. Third edition 2000. Reprinted 2002

Edited, designed and typeset by The Open University

Printed in the United Kingdom by The Burlington Press, Foxton, Cambridge CB2 6SW

ISBN 0 7492 9786 7

Further information on Open University Business School courses may be obtained from the Course Sales Development Centre, The Open University, PO Box 222, Milton Keynes MK7 6YY (Telephone: 01908 653449).

3.4

26999B/b821b4u7i3.4

CONTENTS

1 INTRODUCTION

1.1   INTRODUCTION TO THE BLOCK

Units 7, 8 and 9 form a block which concentrates on a crucial aspect of running an organisation: risk and its management. Bearing in mind the aims of this course, you will not be surprised to find that the lion's share of the material is concerned with financial risk.

However, since it is important not to treat some elements of risk in isolation from their peers, we begin with an essentially strategic technique for analysis: risk mapping. One of the themes of the block is the need for policy-makers to take into account the implications of risk when they are defining the organisation's strategy. This should resonate with memories of your earlier studies of B820 *Strategy*.

Having looked at risk strategically, it is appropriate that we then begin to concentrate on the operational level of the practical management of the various types of financial risk. Unit 7 continues by considering interest rate risk: the risk caused by changes in interest rates. This is a form of risk to which almost all organisations will be exposed at some time or other. It can arise from an organisation's need to raise capital, but also from the management of ordinary operational cash flows. It can even be a serious consideration when an organisation finds itself investing surplus funds rather than itself raising money. Most managers realise the importance of interest rates with regard to the cost of both short- and long-term capital used in their businesses. However, as individuals we are also intimately concerned with this topic when we consider our own savings for the later years of life, be these in the form of pension contributions or other investment methods.

We will look carefully at two main methods of measuring this type of risk, 'gap analysis' and 'duration'. This gets somewhat technical in places, but the required mathematics is not onerous, and in any case it is the concepts, methods and results you need to concentrate on rather than the arithmetic niceties of their derivation. The unit concludes with a discussion of some of the financial products available for managing interest risk.

The first part of Unit 8 ('Foreign exchange and trade risk') concerns itself in some depth with a crucial form of financial risk: foreign exchange risk. As you will know from reading the news over the last few years, mistakes in managing foreign exchange risk can cost a business hundreds of millions of pounds, dollars or euros. But these reported crises are just the tip of the iceberg, and it is probably fair to say that few organisations can claim to optimise their handling of **forex risk**.

As you will see in the unit, it is not sufficient to claim that you are not exposed to foreign exchange risk simply because you are neither an exporter nor an importer. Where do your materials come from? Are they priced on an international market in, say, US dollars? Do your customers export your goods as sub-components in *their* output? Most important of all, who are your *competitors* and what are their cost bases? Forex risk is rather more pervasive than is typically realised.

Unit 8 ends with a discussion of trade or credit risk. We do not intend to turn everyone into loan analysts, but the moment a business allows a customer 'normal trade terms' for payment, it has become a banker providing short-term capital – so it is prudent for its managers to have some exposure to the fundamentals of credit analysis. Fortunately, you have already done the hard part of this in your earlier studies here in B821 – the principles are the same whether you are deciding to invest in a business long-term through equity or short-term as a trade credit provider. The aspects of the income statement and balance sheet you concentrate on differ, but the concepts do not.

Unit 9, 'Contingent risk and policy issues', starts with a study of the field of contingent transactions – 'options' to you and me. The growth of this area is one of the most important developments in practical finance over the last 20 years; it is also one of the least understood. This is a pity, because, as you will read, businesses are almost continually forced to grant (to 'write' in the jargon) options to some of those with whom they transact. In the past, much of this was risk that could not be managed, merely assumed and borne. Options provide a way of managing at least some of this type of risk.

It has to be admitted that the mathematics of option theory is fairly advanced, and the adaptation of theory to the 'messiness' of the real world is still being worked on. Nevertheless, the concepts underlying the calculations are certainly intelligible, as are the techniques for using and managing the products in business. B821 is not primarily a course in financial mathematics, so you will be glad to hear, I am sure, that we can cover the material appropriate to a generalist manager without too much mathematics. The theorists have done so for us, and we have no need to follow their every twist and turn. But if any of you wish to, we can point you in the right direction – *Vital Statistics* will often prove a good starting point.

The block ends with a return to the preoccupation of the early part of Unit 7: the strategic and tactical levels of the management of risk. By now you will have the tools to take the strategic design of the policy-makers and design an operating system, or systems, which implements the strategy and has the best chance of moving towards the goals implicit in it.

Benjamin Franklin said that nothing was certain except death and taxes; Merton Miller revised this in his work on capital structure to debt and taxes. I think they left out one other: risk. But at least we can sometimes do something about risk, and not merely bow to the inevitable!

Aims and objectives of the unit

By the end of this unit, you should be able to:

- understand the general implications of risk for an organisation, and how financial risk types fit into the overall risk situation
- categorise the forms of risk to which an organisation is subject
- plan and carry out a relatively straightforward risk assessment exercise
- make use of the results of a risk mapping exercise

We ought to distinguish immediately between contingent transactions and financial option products. The former, as we will see later, usually involve you granting implicit options to customers; the latter are instruments designed to enable you to hedge such risks.

- understand the concept of interest rate risk
- produce a 'gap chart' for cash and interest risk management purposes
- calculate the 'duration' of a portfolio of cash flows and use the result for quantifying interest rate risk
- understand the concepts behind and basic usage of interest rate products such as forward rate agreements, futures and swaps.

2 RISK ASSESSMENT

In this first working section of the unit we begin by defining more clearly what we mean by 'risk', and then categorise it into its main forms. We then proceed to consider how we might analyse risk – particularly, but not exclusively, **financial risk** – for an organisation, through 'risk mapping'. The section concludes with a look at one example of a template for assessing financial risk specifically.

Having categorised the forms of risk faced by a business, we should consider how such dangers, actual or potential, can be managed. Sometimes this will involve action and sometimes simple awareness and contingency planning so that correction can be applied speedily should an untoward event actually occur.

Risk audit is another term used by some to mean the same as 'risk mapping'. Other people, however, use risk audit more in the sense of a *post hoc* control process. Unfortunately, as yet there is no complete agreement on terminology, but the meaning is usually clear in context.

2.1 DEFINING RISK

How do we define risk? You have already met a couple of empirical definitions in Unit 4, which introduced the concept of variability of stock prices (measured either by the standard deviation, or the beta of the returns of the stock or portfolio) as the idea of risk in the context of portfolio theory. We now extend that into a more comprehensive definition.

The word 'risk' is thought to derive either from the Arabic word *risq* or the Latin word *risicum* (Kedar, 1970). The two possibilities quite neatly combine to give us the meaning for the English term in our context.

The Latin word originally referred to the challenge presented to seafarers by a barrier reef, and so implied a possible negative outcome. The Arabic word, on the other hand, implies 'anything that has been given to you (by God) and from which you draw profit', i.e. connotations of a potential beneficial outcome.

A twelfth-century Greek derivative of the Arabic *risq* related to chance outcomes in general with no implications of positive or negative (Kedar, 1970).

We also combine the two ideas to derive our concept of risk as being 'an *uncertain* future outcome that will improve *or* worsen our position.'

There are three key points about this definition that should be remembered:

1   It is *probabilistic*, i.e. uncertainty is inextricably bound up in it

2   It is *symmetrical* – the outcome may be pleasant or unpleasant

3   It involves *change* – no change, no risk

Strictly speaking, the 'improve or worsen' aspect of the definition does not in itself necessarily imply 'symmetry', by which we usually mean that the 'upside' and 'downside' are of equivalent magnitude. However, for much of financial risk (at least) – which will be the main concern for B821 – risk *is* more or less symmetrical. For example, if one owns some shares, the gain or loss, relative to the purchase price, is the same for a change of 1% in share-price whether it be a profit or a loss – before tax, at least! We will thus keep point 2 in the list above.

BOX 2.1   BUNGEE JUMPING IS RISKY

This may not seem a very controversial idea, but let us use this perhaps lunatic pursuit to illustrate graphically the importance of *uncertainty* to the definition of 'risk' that we will use throughout B821.

If one attaches a length of elastic to one's ankles and then jumps off a very high bridge, it is a risky thing to do. The elastic may be too long; it may stretch excessively; it may snap; or it may work as intended, giving one an adrenaline rush and a thrill like no other.

If one does not jump off the high place, it is not risky – assuming one does not slip or suffer a dizzy spell while looking over the edge.

However, let us also consider another, rather unpleasant, alternative: one jumps off the bridge *without* the bungee cord attached. The situation is *bad* but it is not *risky*. There is no realistic uncertainty as to the outcome.

The Arabic idea of risk is more suitable for buying financial options where, for a fee, you will be certain of the worst case scenario and then expect a positive outcome.

For finance, the 'up- and down-side' definition is more useful, particularly when considering any form of price-movement risk, since prices can (in a free market) fall or rise. Since this type of volatility covers the majority of types of financial risk, we will predominantly use our 'symmetrical' risk definition in this block. However, there is one important exception in finance where it is sensible to think in terms of the 'down-side only' definition: credit risk. When considering credit questions, the *expectation* is that the debt *will* be paid. The only possible unexpected outcome is that we do not get our money, which can hardly be thought of as an 'up-side' possibility! So the Latin idea of risk having negative connotations only is more appropriate in the case of credit.

BOX 2.2   RISK-AVERSION OR THRILL-SEEKING?

Horse-racing might introduce a third possibility where, in the long run, one group always wins (the bookmaker) and the other always loses (the punters)! This may seem a slightly frivolous comment to make within a finance MBA course, but actually it does raise a point we should address before continuing. In business analysis we usually assume that people act in a logical and rational way; this implies that they will only take on avoidable risk if there is the chance of an appropriate reward. They are said to be 'risk-averse', which is the logically sensible stance to take. So how do we reconcile this with the huge amount of empirical evidence given by betting in its various forms that people do *not* always seem to act rationally? In organised gambling it is universally accepted that, overall, the 'house' gains and the customers lose – so is it not irrational for people to gamble?

Risk aversion was covered in Unit 1.

If the potential financial reward was all that was offered, then this would place a serious question-mark against the rationality assumption. In fact, of course, gamblers are human and have other needs as well as financial gain; in this case they are also gaining a qualitative benefit in the 'entertainment' category. People who gamble in a normal way (not necessarily those for whom it has become a compulsion) say that they get pleasure from the added excitement of having a bet on the outcome.

Although it is not easy to measure precisely, it is reasonable to assume that the *combination* of the probable small average expected financial loss with the qualitative excitement benefit is perceived as a net gain by people who gamble. They are still acting rationally overall, if not in purely financial terms.

An example of this is the differing attitudes of the author and a friend to the UK lottery. We both have a scientific background (and an MBA!), so cannot claim to misunderstand the odds; my friend buys one ticket a week – on a Monday for the following Saturday – because he says the mild thrill of a possible (if unlikely!) jackpot is well worth £1 a week. Personally, I don't get any 'buzz' from voluntarily paying 50% tax, so do not play. Thus, I am £52 a year better off, but do not enjoy the thrill on a Saturday night of a gamble and will be 'sick as a parrot' when he scoops a cool £5,000,000.

In business, the organisation is not expected to get 'excited', so only financial return is relevant. Thus the rational expectation of risk aversion is upheld in its strict form, and we *can* use it as an assumption for our risk analysis and management.

Activity 2.1

Before we discuss the risk audit model, please read the article by Ho and Pike, 'The use of risk analysis techniques in capital investment appraisal', in the Course Reader. This should link some of your earlier studies to the themes of Block 4 (Financial Risk Management).

The survey research included in the article was conducted in 1991, but, while the continuing improvement in PC modelling power since then has made for somewhat easier application of the analysis techniques, the basic conclusions of the study still apply today.

For me, the overall impression of the results of the Ho and Pike survey is of the essential pragmatism of managers, which I find reassuring. There is a clear acceptance of the importance of risk analysis and management, but this is tempered by a recognition of the limitations and/or cost effectiveness of the methods available. Similarly, it is apparent that the effort involved in risk analysis is not directly proportional to the size and importance of the capital investment. So while an oil company would be well advised to use many of the available techniques in some detail before developing a new oil field, a small company deciding whether or not to open a new production facility is much more limited in its ability to generate risk information cost-effectively – even though the investment is proportionally just as important to the latter as is the field to the former. But sensitivity analysis on a DCF model is, nowadays, available to any manager with access to any modern spreadsheet program.

As we have seen, many of the problems with implementation are due to complexity rather than any disagreement about applicability or usefulness. Bearing this in mind, we look next at another way of assessing risk – risk mapping. The benefit of this technique compared to some of those covered in the Ho and Pike study is that it can provide information even where a formal, quantitative analysis is infeasible.

2.2 RISK MAPPING

An organisation's attitude towards the various forms of risk to which it is exposed should be a direct interpretation of its strategy. This has implications both ways: the strategy itself must address the appetite and capacity for risk within the business, and the systems and actions of the organisation regarding risk should seek to attain the goals envisaged by the strategy.

'Risk mapping' is used in two related ways: as a general concept, or a specific example of the technique. So 'a risk mapping' could be the output of applying the idea of 'risk mapping'.

As with most aspects of business, this is in practice an iterative process, hopefully improving and adapting over time in the light of experience and information. As an aid to increasing the knowledge within the organisation concerning its risk exposure, it is useful to use the idea of **risk mapping**. This is simply the process of assessing for the organisation as a whole the types and degree of risk to which it is exposed. For some types of risk it is possible to make a reasonably precise and quantitative estimate of the amount of exposure, for others a qualitative judgement may be the best one can do. At this stage of your studies there will also be some forms of risk which you will as yet only be able to assess qualitatively but you will be equipped to deal with these more precisely by the end of the Block – **foreign exchange risk** and **interest rate risk** being two examples.

Whether the assessment is qualitative or quantitative, an organisation ought to be able to come to some conclusion about the relative levels of its various risk elements. This can then be used as an element of information for the formulation of policy, and then for the management implementation of that policy. Thus a 'risk mapping' is more akin to the concept of an internal audit rather than the annual *financial* audit by external accountants; the latter is, essentially, a check that the company's public financial statements are reasonably accurate and not misleading. An internal audit, on the other hand, is principally intended as an investigation of practice with a view to suggesting improvements. So too with a risk mapping.

Another analogy can be made to the idea of a budgetary process. As you will recall from your Stage 1 MBA studies, periodic budget forecasts are usually based on the current situation (incremental budgeting). However, every so often it is a good idea to go 'back to basics' and justify everything from the ground up (zero-based budgeting). A risk mapping process is similar in that, while one should be regularly, or continuously, adjusting one's risk estimates in the light of events, one should also from time to time do a complete assessment as if from the viewpoint of the hypothetical 'independent observer'. This is also the way to conduct an initial risk mapping.

So the idea is conceptually simple: assess and categorise the organisation's risks. However, as with much of finance, the detail is considerably more intricate than the bare statement of principle would imply.

The process can be divided into three sequential activities:

1   Analyse which risk categories are involved.

2   Estimate levels of exposure in terms of size and degree.

3   Rank risks in terms of the importance they should be given when allocating the organisation's risk capacity.

This sequential approach to strategic risk assessment is similar to that in the article by Ho and Pike.

The third activity will usually necessitate an interrogation and interpretation of the overall strategy, and may well also involve a re-assessment of the strategy itself, given that the mapping process may well throw up aspects of risk not at present covered by policy. This is more likely to happen if risk mapping is being performed for the first time, but circumstances change. New elements of risk can appear at any time, and old ones may fade from view. As discussed earlier, the relationship between this type of analysis and strategy should always be seen as an iterative process. A shark – which might well be a risk element in some situations! – must move forward continually if it is not to suffocate. A strategy process, whether driven by corporate sharks or not, ought similarly to aim for continuous progress!

Stage 1 Which risk categories?

There are many different ways in which one could sub-divide risk, so the following list is just one possibility. You may think of your own division if you want to because as long as the categorisation used covers the risk types and is understood by all those using the results, then any chosen scheme is valid.

Our suggestion, therefore, is to use four risk categories, namely:

- Financial
- Organisational
- Market
- Environment

This categorisation is depicted graphically in Figure 2.2 on page 16.

Financial risk refers to possible changes in the monetary value of wealth because of variations in cash balances (i.e. liquidity) or in resources. As you have seen earlier in the course, the conventional approach to risk management is to identify and to assess sources of potential change.

But, stop! Why do we say that you have already learnt about financial risk management? Well, in Units 2 and 4 you learnt about 'gearing' (or 'leverage' in a text of US influence) which identifies the potential of future cash flows not being able to service incremental debt. In this unit you will learn about other potential sources of financial risk and, in particular, that associated with changes in interest rates. Whereas in Unit 8 you will learn about credit risk, cash flow variation and foreign exchange risk. In Unit 9 you will learn about the use of financial options to manage risk.

Let us now continue with our review but only after having one last look at the two forms of gearing; as 'gearing' will not be further discussed in Block 4. See Box 2.3.

BOX 2.3   GEARING: FINANCIAL AND OPERATIONAL

Gearing comes in two forms – financial and operational – but the underlying idea is the same, namely that the ratio between two factors influences the speed with which profit (or loss) varies as revenue changes.

Financial gearing refers to the ratio of debt to equity in the capital structure, which produce a rate-of-change effect on return. Here it is the return *to ordinary shareholders* which is 'geared up' if the proportion of debt increases. If we think of interest payments as a 'fixed-cost' capital charge against operating profits, then what is left over afterwards belongs to the shareholders.

If the percentage rate of operating profit exceeds the interest rate payable on debt capital, the shareholders gain the difference, even though they have not provided that part of the capital base – this increases their equity rate of return. If the operating profit falls short of the interest coverage, then the shareholders lose out. So increased financial gearing speeds up the rate of change of equity profits – up *or* down.

Operational gearing compares the proportion of fixed to variable cost, and is linked to the management accounting concern with '**contribution**'. Note that while the operational gearing is heavily influenced by aspects in the 'organisational' risk category, it is generally regarded as part of 'financial' risk.

Contribution is defined as sales less all variable costs.

In general, a (viable) business with high fixed costs will also have a relatively high contribution-per-unit rate. Thus as sales volume increases, large losses associated with high uncovered fixed costs decrease rapidly, then – once fixed costs are overcome – profits accumulate rapidly. This is said to be high operational gearing.

In contrast, a company with low operational gearing will have relatively small fixed costs to cover, but the rate of increase of profits beyond break-even will be comparatively slow. This is a low-risk, low-return scenario.

A pair of break-even diagrams which should clarify the difference between the two situations is shown in Figure 2.1.

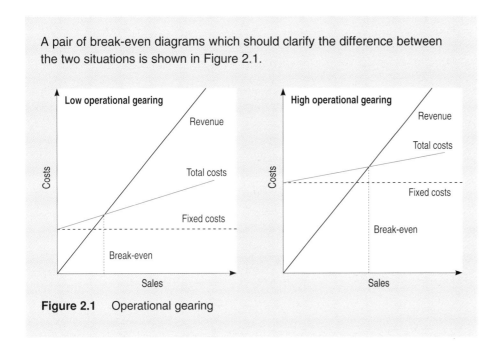

Figure 2.1   Operational gearing

As can be seen from Box 2.3, gearing is an element of risk because it affects the overall rate of return achieved for a given level of sales. In normal conditions financial gearing is under the conscious control of the senior management – they can *choose* a debt/equity ratio – but **operational gearing** is typically partially conditioned by the nature of the business. For example, a market 'fruit and veg.' business will tend to have low fixed costs but also low contribution rates, whereas an electricity generating company will, necessarily, be subject to the high capital costs involved with building power stations. Nevertheless, good management can in both cases influence operational gearing, particularly choosing to run with *higher* operational gearing than the business type demands, for example, investing in high levels of automation to make the process more efficient.

In our list we also identified *organisational risk*. This category aims to cover all elements which impinge on the creation of organisational products. So, operational risk would include factors such as industrial relations, labour costs, skill requirements and others associated with 'personnel'. My definition would also include the quality and price of materials, supplier power, potential disruption of supply and other issues associated with 'materials'. I would include a sub-category for managing 'processes' to capture issues around safety, production efficiency, process improvement, and so on. Finally, I would include R&D as 'organisational' because I would distinguish between actual development of a product from the marketing analysis which has identified the opportunity.

A potential overlap is between 'process' (and possibly 'R&D') and operational gearing in the 'financial' category, inasmuch as changes in process – for good or ill – may affect the ability of management to alter the operational gearing level. Similarly, if one regards labour costs as closer to fixed than variable costs, then a change to staffing levels may also influence the operational gearing.

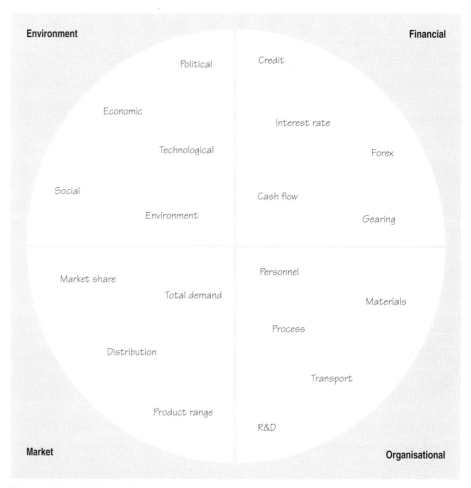

Figure 2.2   Risk mapping categories

See the Glossary if you would like a reminder of the definitions of market risk and specific risk.

Market risk would be concerned with externally-oriented factors which impinge directly on the business' sales. In practice one could also define it as the risk elements which should be the responsibility of the marketing function, therefore some sub-divisions could be: 'market share', 'total demand', 'distribution', and 'product range'.

Finally, you could identify sources of risk which are industry-specific through a formal analysis of the competitive *environment*. There is a logical and intentional similarity here with the headings you will have met in STEP analysis (or PEST, depending on the author) earlier on your MBA studies. So no need for me to elaborate any further.

PEST = Social, Technological, Economic and Political.

As you can see, risk mapping is not meant to 're-invent the wheel' but to build upon other methods from your MBA 'toolbox'. Further, you should have been noticing as you have been reading that much of your study of strategy has bearing upon the analysis of risk; for example, Porter's 'five forces' and 'value chain' models help to illuminate an organisation's risk profile in most cases. As we will discuss shortly, decisions about a company's appetite for risk – both in absolute and relative ways – are fundamentally a strategic function. The application of risk management techniques may be regarded as operational or tactical, but the goals must derive directly from strategic deliberation.

Stage 2 Estimating risk

Having identified and agreed the categorisation appropriate to the organisation, the following task is measuring the assorted risks.

There are two main ways of thinking about the possible results of risk exposure. Either one can focus on the 'expected return' or upon 'outcome v. return'. The 'expected return' method is usually easier to use in a quantitative or comparative way. For example, assume one is faced with choosing between action A or action B; if it is possible to calculate the expected return of the alternatives, then it is usually sensible to opt for whichever offers the better expected return.

How does one calculate expected return? As described in Unit 1, it is the sum of the values of the return of each possible outcome multiplied by its probability of occurrence. Formulaically this is represented as:

$$E(R) = \sum_{i=1}^{i=n} p_i R_i$$

Where

> $E(R)$ = expected return
>
> R_i = value of outcome i
>
> p_i = probability of outcome i.

This is the same definition as that for the mean return in statistics, which is fortunate since 'expected return' and 'mean return' are the same thing!

An important use for expected return is when considering **avoidable risk**, i.e. risk to which the organisation can choose whether or not to be exposed. The idea of risk aversion is invoked with avoidable risk, and expected return gives us a decision rule to apply in such circumstances. The simplest form of the rule is:

> 'Only take on avoidable risk if the expected return is *positive*.'

Similarly, if one has to decide between choices, the rule should be:

> 'Choose the option with the *highest* expected return.'

You should immediately realise that either form of this rule is not yet complete as it does not address the balance between *level* of risk and *level* of return. Strictly speaking, satisfying the rule as so far stated is a *necessary* but not a *sufficient* condition for accepting avoidable risk. Please accept this for the moment, as it avoids judgements about 'acceptable' return for taking on risk; the simplification will allow us to investigate, in Box 2.4, another aspect of deciding about risk exposure.

The expected return method is very much applicable and useful in finance. For instance, in your study of portfolio theory in Unit 4.

BOX 2.4   WHEN SIMPLICITY IS NOT ENOUGH

You have the chance to play one of two coin-tossing games. Whichever you choose to play (if at all), you will only have the chance to toss once. Oh yes, notwithstanding the reputation of your opponent, the coin *is* fair!
So the probability of a head = probability of a tail = 0.5.

Game A: If the coin lands on heads you will receive £12; if it comes up tails, you pay £10.

Game B: If the coin lands on heads you will receive £12,500, if it comes up tails, you pay £10,000.

What should you do? First, calculate the expected return of each game:

Game A: E(R) = (+£12 × 0.5) + (−£10 × 0.5) = +£1

Game B: E(R) = (+£12,500 × 0.5) + (−£10,000 × 0.5) = +£1,250

So you play Game B? It offers £1,249 more expected return. It even offers a better percentage return, i.e.

Game A: E(R)/'stake' = £1/£10 = +10%

Game B: E(R)/'stake' = £1,250/£10,000 = +12.5%

The simple decision rule is quite clear: play Game B.

But what if you lose on your one toss?

Personally, I could not afford the loss of £10,000, and I doubt if many of you could either. The possible negative outcome is not supportable, so I must decline to play Game B even though the expected return is very favourable.

So the simple rule needs to be extended to include checking that the 'downside' possibilities are not 'catastrophic' if they actually occur.

Now, I *can* afford to 'invest' £10 in Game A ...

This idea of *avoiding catastrophic outcomes* leads us to the second factor we need to include when assessing risk, namely 'possible outcome v. return'. This does not contradict the 'risk v. return' as epitomised by portfolio theory and CAPM, but adds to it. 'Risk v. return' looks at the situation as a whole and judges whether *on average* the risk is worth accepting. This new criterion says that for some sorts of risk one must *also* consider whether some possible outcomes are so insupportable as to outweigh almost any level of *average* return.

Note that you have already met this idea of 'average risk' when studying portfolio theory and the CAPM. You measured it in terms of standard deviations of the returns. Standard deviation is a way of condensing into one number information about the average amount of scatter around the mean of a distribution. Since this represents uncertainty about the return one receives in any particular period, it is truly a measure of risk as we have defined it. However, for some types of risk it is not practical to calculate a proper statistical measure such as standard deviation, or one may feel that insupportable outcomes represent 'discontinuities' not completely captured by a historic measure based on past returns. For example, stock market declines may be seen as included in and allowed for by standard deviation. But crashes, such as in 1929 and 1987, reflect such radical and unusual changes as to preclude capture in such a measure.

In either situation, including a 'catastrophe avoidance' criterion is not a rival to standard deviation but an adjustment to it.

Figure 2.3 overleaf illustrates the idea, perhaps rather crudely. Scenario A shows the value of a project for the whole range of possible outcomes; it is not a true 'distribution' in the proper statistical sense, but is meant to represent qualitatively the same sort of idea. The project is more likely than not to end up with a positive value, as implied by E(R) > 0; furthermore, all the possibilities give relatively modest values, some positive, some negative, none extreme.

Scenario B, on the other hand, is *expected* to give a higher value than A, but there is a small but finite chance of it ending up horribly negative, a 'catastrophic' outcome. So while the expected return is better, we should also include in our consideration the very nasty possibility.

It is worth noting that the 'expected return' system can encompass the 'possible outcome v. return' method. If one looks at the table used to calculate each of the terms in the E(R) summation, as well as the final result, then one can analyse the individual outcomes as required for the second method. Here one considers each potential outcome and what would be the profit/loss should it actually occur. If one or more outcomes have an unacceptably large negative return, i.e. a 'catastrophic' result, then this item of information should be taken into account.

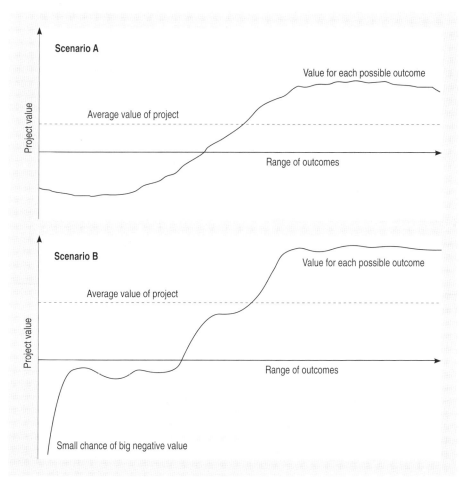

Figure 2.3 'Expected return' and 'possible catastrophe'

BOX 2.5 DRUNKARDS AND CANALS

This seemingly imprecise idea of 'catastrophic outcome' is just as mathematically rigorous as the ideas underlying the 'risk and return' view of portfolio theory. In fact, it is the *same* probability technique, but with an added constraint.

In Unit 1, you were introduced to the idea of risk and return being based on a probability distribution of possible outcomes. Often in finance we find that returns are normally distributed, particularly when considering stock markets – as in portfolio theory. Such distributions can be represented as 'drunkard's walks', i.e. whether step (n+1) goes 'left' or 'right' is independent of what happened at step n.

See random walk theory in Unit 1 and the Glossary.

> Adding the possibility of catastrophic outcomes can be modelled simply by setting a level from which, if reached, one can never recover. In business terms this could represent bankruptcy; to a mathematician, it simply means her 'drunkard' has fallen into the canal ...
>
> The point is that our new criterion is an elaboration not a contradiction of what has gone before.

A benefit of this 'summing over outcomes' method is that it forces us to think through the consequences of each possibility; sometimes this is more important than calculating expected value. Also, it is much easier to apply this system where the assessment must be essentially qualitative, either in respect of the values or of the probabilities. However, this method has one significant disadvantage: if it does not result in comparable measures, it makes assessing between alternatives much more difficult, or, at the very least, less precise.

Activity 2.2

The NPV rule of 'accept projects with positive NPV' seems to be an example of the naive version of our risk rule, i.e. without considering the level of return. Is this true?

No – providing the cost of capital has been correctly risk-weighted. Assuming that this has been done, then a zero NPV means that the project is exactly 'fair'. In the terms of this risk discussion, the expected return is just enough to justify the risk. If the calculation was done with a company's 'standard' discount rate, the NPV rule has potentially been impoverished as a decision tool, especially if the proposed project is much riskier or much safer than the average for the business.

We are usually concerned with the product of outcome *and* probability of occurrence, so we need not include remote possibilities, simply restrict ourselves to events with a reasonable chance of occurring.

A real world example may help to illustrate this idea of avoiding catastrophe by identifying problems in advance (see Box 2.6). Unfortunately, as you will see, it does not also demonstrate the 'low probability' aspect as the failure was in fact entirely predictable! A London bank lost a considerable amount of money over the deal.

BOX 2.6   JUST GO LOOK ...

A project under the auspices of the World Bank was instigated to build a large industrial factory 'up country' in a very under-developed part of East Africa. The project appraisal was very carefully done in Washington, the NPV looked good; two World Bank employees even went to the client country to meet the relevant government officials and assess the project's viability.

The World Bank decided to go ahead with its part of the deal, which was essentially to finance the development of the land. The British bank financed the export from the UK of the complete plant and machinery; the goods were shipped to Africa and the exporter was paid.

Three years later the machinery was still on the coast, and was effectively scrap metal. The loan, of the order of a few million pounds, was a near total write-off.

What had gone wrong? The World Bank evaluators met all their government and business counterparts – in the country's capital. They were not themselves going to risk an uncomfortable and possibly dangerous trip 'out there'. So they never found out that there was a 50 mile stretch on the route between the coast and the factory with simply no road. It was physically impossible – and always had been – to transport heavy plant and machinery to the required location.

In fact, using our definition of risk, it was not the project that was 'risky' as envisaged. It was a 'dead cert' catastrophe. The risk was in relying on other people's analysis, and a reluctance actually to 'go look'...

What your risk mapping does need to show are the key areas of risk for the organisation in terms of the degree of 'danger' and the size of the exposure. The aim is to provide input data to enable informed strategic decision-making about allocating the company's risk capacity.

Where possible, it is useful if the mapping includes benchmarks for at least some of the risk types. In practice this is more likely to be feasible for 'market-oriented' risks (e.g. foreign exchange, interest rate, commodity price, etc.) as there is more chance of there being a published measure against which your own situation can be judged. In any case, provision of such information to the extent possible will usually help senior management's decision-making.

It is beyond the scope of this unit to go into great detail concerning methods for technical analysis of general types of risk – specific forms of financial risk measurement, such as for foreign exchange or interest rate, will be described in relevant parts of this Block. But as an example, Box 2.7 shows the operational research technique of decision tree analysis, which can be useful for showing the linkage between and implications of making choices. Even if you do not go through the whole process of estimation and 'roll back', just drawing the tree will often clarify the cause and effect of sequential decisions.

BOX 2.7   THE CONCEPT OF 'DECISION TREES'

The principle in this operations research technique is to draw a graph of decision points and outcomes for a project or process, which forms the 'tree' and its branches. In the full method, a monetary value and probability is assigned to each outcome and then the tree is 'rolled back' to work out the pathway through the project which offers the highest 'expected monetary value' (EMV). An example is shown in Figure 2.4 for a TV company deciding about producing a new series.

See also *Vital Statistics*, Section 1.3.2.

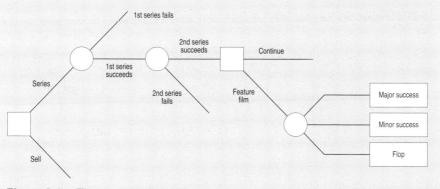

Figure 2.4   The concept of decision trees

For those interested, the full example with values, probabilities and 'roll back' is shown in Appendix 1. Here I wish only to suggest the use of the technique in a risk-analysis context.

Often just going through the process of drawing the tree is useful in itself. In particular, it helps clarify where our choices branch away from each other, in other words if we choose to do X we have 'burnt our boats' with respect to choices W, Y and Z. Clearly, the points at which we cut ourselves off from possible courses of action are significant when thinking about the risks of a project. The graphical form can at times be in itself a direct help by showing us where, for example, re-ordering of the project could serve to delay irreversible decisions – often an immediate aid to risk reduction.

Adding in the values and probabilities is, in effect, providing the input for an 'expected return' calculation but in a way which also takes into account the chronological sequence of events. Sometimes this adds little to one's decision-making; but often with more complicated projects (or strategic plans if considering a whole organisation) it *does* improve the manager's knowledge to a worthwhile degree – and that ought, on average, to lead to better choices being made.

The idea of considering business choices ties in with the concept of 'real options' that you met in Unit 5, and the Dixit and Pindyck article in the Course Reader.

As you have seen in Units 1 and 4, and earlier in this section, standard deviation is very often the key measure for financial risks.

We will discuss scenario analysis in Unit 9 as it is really more pertinent to policy-*setting* than to analysis of the present risk situation.

So what should be the output from this second stage of the risk mapping process? Against each category chosen in stage 1 there should be an analysis, probably containing both numeric and qualitative information, assessed in whatever way is appropriate for the particular risk-type. This should cover the following points:

1   *Why exposed* – Is the exposure unavoidable? Bear in mind that, in the long run, all risks are avoidable. Scenario analysis may show how certain risks *can* be avoided, or minimised, if different choices are made.

2   *Size of exposure* – This certainly needs to be assessed on a relative basis (i.e. what proportion of total risk does this element represent) but if an absolute value can be placed on it, so much the better. It is often as useful to senior management to use a rating scale as to put actual numbers, provided the scale is understandable and can be sufficiently discriminating. For example, grading 1 to 10, giving a percentage, 'extreme'/'very high'/ ... /'low' etc.
For comparison purposes, it is important to use (as much as is possible) the same grading system throughout.

3   *Warnings* – The analysis should flag any potential catastrophic outcomes arising from a particular risk element. Where feasible, it is helpful if the analysis shows what is currently done to avoid or ameliorate a mischance; alternatively, suggestions for future action can be included.

4   *Cost of risk* – If the risk is avoidable, what would be the cost of so doing? What is the potential benefit?

This 'correlation of risk' is clearly akin to portfolio theory. However, because here we are considering a much broader range of risk-types it is not possible to be as mathematically precise as in portfolio theory but the idea is the same.

5   *Correlations of risk* – If there are key risk elements that are correlated, it is helpful to make plain the linkage. As many risk types are interrelated, the link need only be made explicit when it is thought to be important – or you will be linking everything to everything else.

The overall goal for the mapping should be kept in mind: providing risk information to the organisation's policy-makers. So the trick is, as always, to end up with as succinct a report as is consistent with giving the senior management the input needed for them to produce an appropriate definition of corporate strategy.

Stage 3 Allocating risk capacity

The third and final stage of the mapping is meant to put a form of rank order on to the risks previously identified as to facilitate the allocation of risk capacity. The ease of accomplishing this depends considerably upon the care with which stage 2 has been undertaken; it may simply require a summary of the information already produced – but it may not always prove so simple.

A categorisation hierarchy which typically proves fruitful for this part of the analysis is:

    A   Unavoidable risk associated with core activities

    B   Risk unavoidable except by ceasing non-core activity

    C   Avoidable risk, core activities

    D   Avoidable risks, non-core activities

    E   Selectable risk

"'Be careful!' All you can tell me is 'be careful'!"

The intention is to help the policy-makers by giving a sequence for consideration, i.e. Group A 'uses up' some of the risk capacity before one can consider B to E, and so on.

Group E needs some clarification; it is the set for types of risk where the degree of risk can be adjusted more or less voluntarily without changing the operations of the business. The classic example would be financial gearing – the management can, at least in the medium term, choose the debt/equity ratio without altering the company's activities.

Some risk elements can appear in both group E *and* elsewhere. For example, it may be necessary to accept some foreign exchange risk as a concomitant to doing business (Group C) but the organisation could also take on forex risk that was essentially speculative – that part would be Group E. In effect, Group E can be regarded as a 'balancing item' between the total risk represented by the main business and the capacity for risk decided upon as acceptable by the management. Assuming, of course, that the former is smaller than the latter ...

It is a good idea where possible to rank the risk factors *within* the groups, but how possible this is depends on the measures used. If the expected value and standard deviation method is predominant, then ordering is feasible; most financial risks are amenable to this way of measuring risk/return, but whether the same is true of organisational, market and environmental risk types is less predictable. Ranking may also be possible with a scaled system, but this will often depend on the degree of discrimination the chosen scale allows. In general, the ordering is aiming to put at the top of each group's list the factors with the best risk/return profile, and the worst at the bottom.

If two factors, A and B, have the same risk assessment, perhaps measured by standard deviation, but A offers a better expected return, then the ordering is straightforward. It is less easy to be precise if A is also riskier; at this point the organisation's particular attitude to risk becomes important. A very conservative business will require more return per unit of additional risk than will a more adventurous one, assuming the terms 'conservative' and 'adventurous' refer to the degree of risk-aversion of the respective organisations. The rankings must reflect this individual risk-attitude.

Another way of partitioning within the groups is to treat linked risks together. For example, if there is a set of risks all associated with operating in a particular country, report them together, on the premise that strategic-level management may only be able to act on them as a group anyway. This form of partitioning can be used as well as, rather than instead of, the ranking procedure, but this may add more complication than illumination to senior management's interpretation. It can only be decided upon on a case-by-case basis.

By now you should have a sizeable report on the organisation's overall risk profile – and hopefully a better understanding of that profile. It is time for decision-making to take over from analysis.

2.3   ASSESSING THE RESULTS

A risk mapping is but one input to policy-making. It is usually an important element, but can only be useful when put in context with other strategic requirements.

This is not the place to repeat your studies on strategy, so let us just look at the use of the mapping in the direct strategic aspect of risk policy-setting. In practice, risk is also a consequence of other policy decisions, so the following should be seen in context rather than in isolation.

It is reasonable to believe that an organisation has an intrinsic capacity for absorbing risk, dependent on such factors as its size, its economic and/or social role, the attitude of the owners, etc.

Unfortunately, it is seldom easy to put a figure on that capacity for any particular organisation, though there is often a consensus about the 'ballpark' area for the total. For example, most people would expect to see a bio-technology company accepting more risk than, say, a charity providing housing for disadvantaged people. But deciding whether, for example, cancer relief has more risk capacity than the British Heart Foundation would be much more difficult, if not impossible.

However, in the corporate world – especially for exchange-listed companies – while saying what *is* the risk capacity for a business is still fraught with difficulty, the market will be very clear if it thinks a company has got it wrong. Too much risk and the share price declines or even collapses, too little (i.e. excessive unused capacity) and a take-over bid may appear – nowadays, often a highly leveraged bid, using the excess risk capacity on offer.

Let us assume that the board has, by some process (which will necessarily include evaluation of other strategic decisions already made), decided upon an acceptable level of total risk, how should policy formulation proceed?

It is important that risk allocation be seen as a *constraint* on the system, not a *driver*. By this we mean that it is the other inputs to strategy – corporate goals, market opportunities, core industry, etc. – which should be promoting the direction of the company. The risk mapping and risk capacity calculations should be used to 'keep score' so that the organisation does not overstep the mark. However, the effect of different parts of a business acting like a portfolio may mean that simply adding up the risks of individual aspects of the organisation will over-state the net risk. This can be allowed for in the mapping process (with some difficulty) or it may be allowed for in a less precise way by senior management having taken a somewhat optimistic view of the total risk capacity of the business (i.e., an over-estimate of risk capacity compensating for an over-estimate of the net risk).

In practice, the information made available by the mapping can help do more than just ensure that the business does not step over the risk cliff into the chasm of destruction. Mapping can assist in the choice of path so that the direction taken heads most swiftly towards the organisation's goals, without smashing on the rocks or meandering inefficiently. By clarifying what dangers face the business, risk mapping better enables management to avoid them without having to leave an excessive 'margin for error'. The likelihood of optimising the risk to return equation is maximised.

Activity 2.3 _____

Listen to Audio Programme 4 'Risk mapping'. It is a conversation with two managers responsible for general risk assessment within their respective organisations. Philip Thomas works for Bass plc, a UK brewing and leisure group, and Paul Hopkin is Head of Risk Management for the BBC.

They are not finance specialists, and talk rather more generally about risk assessment than has been covered in this section. Nevertheless, I hope you find the discussion with them helps to illustrate some of the material you have just been studying, and that it shows that the process of risk mapping is more than just an academic exercise.

2.4   A TEMPLATE FOR FINANCIAL RISK ANALYSIS

The preceding sub-sections have of necessity been generalised, since they have had to be reasonably applicable to a variety of risk-types. With financial risk, however, we can do rather better. In the rest of Block 4 we will cover a wide range of techniques and products for identifying and managing various forms of financial risk, but before doing so we can give ourselves a more precise 'template' for thinking about financial risk.

The following material takes the template from 'The Business of Finance: a treasury policy blueprint', written for the Association of Corporate Treasurers by David Swann and John Precious. The complete text is accessible through the B821 website (See Activity 2.4), and you may want to have a look at parts of it when convenient for you to do so. This sub-section is drawn from the first chapter, which concerns company-wide financial risk analysis.

To keep this discussion reasonably short, I am going to reproduce their 'top level' template only and then the 18 questions they recommend asking while undertaking an analysis of an organisation's financial risk. Each of the questions is explained neatly in their paper, together with examples from companies.

The template considers the 'contributions, limitations and expectations' of nine 'stakeholder' types across five risk elements, namely:

- Foreign exchange rates
- Interest rates
- Commodity prices
- Equity and funding
- Company-specific factors

The complete 'grid' is shown in Table 2.1.

Table 2.1 A 'financial risk map' (Swann and Precious template)					
	Forex rate	Interest rate	Commodity price	Equity & funding	Company-specific
Shareholders					
Structure/management of company					
Customers					
Suppliers					
Competitors					
Regulators					
Banks/debt providers					
Tax authorities					
Others ...					

The column headings are similar to but not identical with the five sub-categories in our own framework (see Figure 2.2). Why the differences? Partly because Swann and Precious are only covering financial risk. For example, they include 'commodity price' as a financial category, whereas in our model it would come into 'materials' in the organisational group. In a similar way, our 'gearing' would be encapsulated in their 'equity and funding'; 'credit' and 'cash flow' would be spread across all five of their categories. Which view is 'better' or 'right'? Neither, they are simply different, approaching the problem from slightly differing viewpoints. Swann and Precious are writing for the Association of Corporate Treasurers, and their model is aimed at a somewhat different audience from B821 students. What is important is whether or not each model is sufficient and complete in its own right.

How would one fill in the various cells of the grid? Typically, with a qualitative summary (i.e. words!) of how the particular risk category influences or is influenced by the stakeholder to which the relevant row refers. Where possible, one would include a quantitative estimate, but this is not necessarily easy, nor particularly helpful for some of the stakeholder categories. However, for 'shareholders', 'company' and 'debt providers', giving some form of relative estimate (perhaps a percentage of overall risk, represented by each risk category) can be helpful to senior management. It will necessarily be an approximation but can nevertheless be a useful aid for strategic-level decision-making.

Let us look at the list of questions in the Swann and Precious model, because it provides an excellent comprehensive *aide-mémoire* for performing a risk analysis, audit, or mapping irrespective of how one chooses to categorise the results.

- What risks do the principal shareholders believe to be inherent in the business? Do the shareholders want the company to retain these risks or do they want them managed or reduced?

- What is the risk propensity of the Board? Does it believe that all risks should be hedged or are some regarded as just another business risk? What are the overall financial objectives of the company?

- To whom does the company sell? Where are the customers centred and what are their base currencies? Do the customers understand the financial risks they face?

- Who makes the sale to the customer? Are goods sold centrally or locally? What are the implications of any internal transfer pricing practices?

- Where are the company's manufacturing centres? How easy is it to switch locations? Is there an overlap between the main currencies of cost and of income?

- What materials are used in the manufacturing process? Is the company subject to price or volume quotas on some materials? Are some processes energy-dependent?

- Where are the company's suppliers based? Are their financial risks priced implicitly into the products they sell?

- What are the standard terms of business? Is the business essentially short term or has it long timescales? Is the business cyclical? Is it possible to forecast the cash flows for the chosen periods?

- Are non-standard contractual terms used with some customers or suppliers? Are currency variation clauses used to the detriment of the company?

- Where are the company's competitors based? In what currencies do they sell? In what currencies do they buy? What are their **hedging** policies?

- What is the company's reaction to tax or accounting driven financial risk management strategies?

- What are the long term cash requirements of the company? What are the current levels and locations of committed funding and facilities? Are acquisitions or divestments planned? Are there major product or market developments planned?

- What is the size and structure of the banking group serving the company's needs? What is the state of the relationship between the company and the banks? What financial covenants are there on the existing bank (and any other) debt?

- Is the company rated by an external credit rating agency? What are the company's expectations of the risk management approach?

- Are significant assets held overseas?

- Are cash balances held in subsidiaries at home or overseas? Are these structural cash surpluses or do balances fluctuate? Are long and short cash positions matched by inter-company loans?

- Does the company hold any equity-based investments?
- How are the company's sales affected by economic conditions?

Swann and Precious (1996)

The authors then point out that the list 'is certainly not exhaustive'! Clearly, the questions cover many risk types which I have classified into non-financial categories. This is not unreasonable, given that Swann and Precious do not have the other three groups; they therefore 'spread' financial risk to include other aspects of risk.

The list is also relentlessly 'private sector', indeed quite strongly oriented towards manufacturing, but most of the questions can be usefully and easily adapted for service industries, not-for-profit or public-sector organisations.

Activity 2.4 _____

Read 'Performing a company-wide financial risk analysis' in the Swann and Precious' paper. As mentioned earlier, it is available through the B821 website.

Activity 2.5 _____

Think about your own organisation and how you would answer the questions in the list for it. Which ones are relevant (even if you personally do not have enough information to answer them)? Does the relevant/ irrelevant grouping say anything about your firm? Keep in mind that the questions are intended to assist you in filling in the Swann and Precious template in Table 2.1.

SUMMARY

This has been a long and quite detailed section, but it boils down to answering two questions: what types of risk and how much risk is the organisation exposed to?

Risk encompasses such a broad range of possibilities that it is not possible to give a definitive method of measurement appropriate in all cases; one must apply different methodologies to different categories of risk. However, it is realistic to try wherever possible to use some form of the 'expected value' technique. For some types of risk one can do this strictly quantitatively but for others one may need to include some qualitative scaling system.

Fortunately, financial risk is a category which is typically amenable to quantitative analysis; this is generally more precise than qualitative analysis and measurement is easier to automate with computer applications. Thus it is practical to consider tracking financial risk continuously, rather than relying on a periodic 'mapping'.

The section provided one possible system for categorising risk, but it is important to remember that there is nothing special about the groupings used. The crucial point is that any system used should be comprehensive while remaining useful as a way of summarising the organisation's risk profile. Indeed, because the suggested set of categories is necessarily generalised, given the subject of this unit, it is probable that you would be able to produce a set better attuned to the situation facing your particular organisation. Nevertheless, our model does represent a good starting point for adapting to any individual case.

The model breaks down 'risk mapping' into three stages:

1   What risk categories?

2   Estimating risk

3   Allocating risk capacity

The first two are essentially technical processes, while the third stage conflates analysis and policy-making. In this section we concentrated on the former, discussing how to rank the risk estimates better to inform the strategic function of setting risk policy. The latter will be discussed at the end of this Block, in Unit 9.

We concluded with a template for undertaking a financial risk analysis. In practice, the related list of questions produces information about aspects of risk other than financial as defined in the earlier model. The template can, therefore, be seen as giving a reasonably general *aide-mémoire* for undertaking a risk mapping, whatever your choice of categorisation.

3 INTEREST RATE RISK

Having completed the strategic-level risk mapping, let us come down for the rest of this Block to the tactical/operational level and concentrate on the category of risk which is the main concern of B821: financial risk. There is no implication that this aspect is any more or less important than the other risk types, simply that the study of their management is the responsibility of other MBA courses.

In particular, as we mentioned earlier, your studies of strategy in B820 should have equipped you to take this material and place it in the wider context of business. As a manager you should always bear in mind that the actions you take regarding risk management within your own area of responsibility will send ripples throughout the organisation (and other peoples' ripples will, in turn, affect you). Hopefully, the preceding work on risk mapping will have reminded you of this; it is all too easy to end up concentrating on one's own sphere of influence so that one forgets to interpret how it interacts with everyone else's.

In this section we define interest rate risk, which is the subject of the rest of this unit.

Before discussing interest rate risk, let us just remind ourselves of the five sub-categories of financial risk, and about where in the Block each will be covered.

- *Gearing* – discussed in Section 2 and Unit 4
- *Interest rate* – Sections 3 to 7
- *Foreign exchange* – Unit 8
- *Credit* – Unit 8
- *Cash flow* – Unit 8

3.1   INTEREST RATE RISK

Interest rate risk is the risk of gain or loss from the rise or fall of interest rates. This is of great importance, as all organisations are, at some time or another, lenders or borrowers; in fact most businesses are both at all times.

Furthermore, as you have already seen from your study of the CAPM, interest rates influence directly the cost of all forms of equity capital as well, so the topic is considerably broader in reach than just debt provision.

At the end of this section we will be able to give a quantified enhancement of this definition of interest rate risk, but for the present it is sufficient to realise it is the gain or loss caused by interest rate changes.

Another aspect of the importance of interest risk in our lives is in our roles as long-term investors. It is reasonable to assume that most B821 students pay into a pension fund, or some other form of long-term savings. Interest exposure should, therefore, be of significant interest. On the other side of the coin, many of us have exposure also as borrowers, typically having passed through the SLINKy and DINKy stages of life to be drinking deep as HEMLOKs.

SLINKy = Single, Lavish Income, No Kids,
DINKy = Dual Incomes, No Kids
– and HEMLOKs = Huge Expensive Mortgage, Lots Of Kids ...

From the viewpoint of an investor in debt instruments, the potential for exposure is obvious, but the implications of interest risk are of concern to others besides loan providers. For example, equity investors are concerned about interest rates, as one component in the estimation of a 'fair' return on equity capital is the prevailing interest rate – remember the CAPM formula from Unit 4.

The *users* of capital are also fundamentally concerned about interest risk as it affects the cost of raising funds. Granted, once a business has raised an amount of debt capital at a fixed rate, the service cost of that particular liability will not change for the life of the agreement – but what happens when the time comes to refinance the borrowing? Also, floating rate debt rates and required rates of return for equity change rapidly as interest rates vary.

So interest rate risk is a topic which should be of concern to all people. However, for much of this section we will be analysing interest risk from the point of view of an investor in debt, particularly fixed-rate debt; this is simply because the points to be considered are easier to see in the world of fixed cash flows happening at pre-ordained times, which is the arena of **bonds**. Box 3.1 gives a reminder of the definition of a government bond that you met in Unit 1, so it should be familiar.

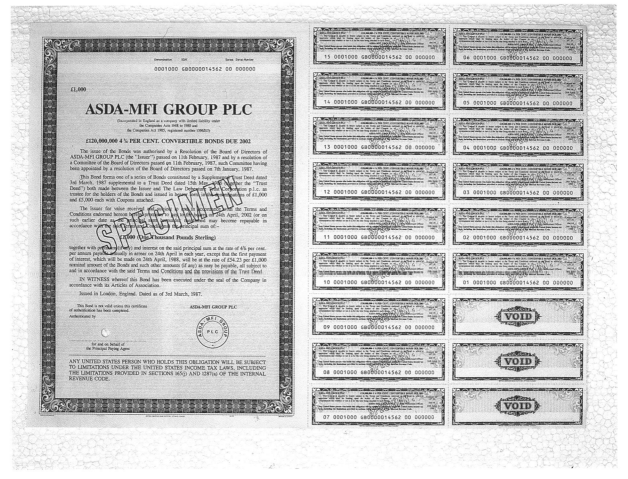

A Eurobond with its interest coupons

BOX 3.1   WHAT IS A BOND?

In essence a bond is a medium or long-term, **securitised** evidence of indebtedness issued by a state, supra-state (e.g. the World Bank, Asian Development Bank) or corporate entity.

Typically a corporate bond will have an initial **maturity** of between 5 and 15 years, a government issue between 3 and 30 years; for shorter maturities other debt products are available, and the upper limit is set by what investors will accept rather than by any regulation. For example, UK Consols are 'perpetuals' – they have no fixed repayment date – and in 1996 Disney Corporation launched and sold a 100-year bond, though more for the publicity value than because they had a century-long project in mind!

A majority of bonds are issued on a 'fixed-rate' basis, paying a known rate of interest throughout their life, but 'floating rate' is also common. The latter are called, quite logically, Floating Rate Notes or 'FRNs'; some bonds even pay returns linked to a given indicator. For example, UK Index-linked Gilts are calculated by reference to the Retail Price Index, the country's key inflation indicator.

'Securitised' means the bond is issued in a freely transferable form, but this can either be 'registered' or 'bearer' in form. With the former, the issuer maintains a registration of ownership (similar to the registration of equities); for the latter, the borrower will pay interest and **principal** to whomsoever turns up with the right piece of paper, giving anonymity to holders. Most domestic government bonds and some domestic corporate markets use registered issues (e.g. the US corporate bond market, by law), but the international and Euro-markets typically issue bonds in bearer form.

In the markets and the press, bonds are usually described by a name of a form similar to:

$$\text{XYZ } 6^{3}/_{4} \text{ 2009}$$

i.e. XYZ corporate bond paying 6.75% interest, maturing in 2009. Most bonds repay all the principal at maturity – a 'bullet' repayment – and pay interest either annually (e.g. eurobonds) or semi-annually (e.g. US Treasuries).

Interest payments are called 'coupons' because the bonds themselves really do have tear-off coupons that the investor presents to the issuer for each individual interest payment. In practice this is done automatically by the investors' agents who keep the bonds in safe custody – for eurobonds very often one of the two main clearing houses, Euroclear or CEDEL. Similarly, when buying or selling a eurobond, more often than not both parties will maintain accounts with Euroclear or CEDEL, and so the transfer becomes simply a book entry, with the securities themselves staying safe in the clearing house's vaults.

How does one value a fixed-rate bond? It consists of a known set of cash flows payable at known dates, so the price of a bond is simply the value today of the sum of its future cash flows: the present value. Alternatively, one may want to look at the percentage return offered by the bond, for which the IRR is used (called the 'yield to maturity' (YTM) or 'redemption yield' in the bond markets). Note that the DCF formula for a bond can only have one real IRR (because it consists, for investors, simply of an initial negative and then several positive cash flows), so one important worry about IRR is not relevant here.

In the USA short term government debt is called 'T- bills'. 'T-notes' are those of medium term maturity (i.e. 3 to 5 years) and 'T bonds' are those of long term maturity (30 years); where the 'T' stands for 'Treasury Department'.

The calculations to find the yield to maturity are in Section 5.4.1 of *Vital Statistics*.

Prices are usually quoted with 100 representing 100% of face value, so if a bond with a face value of £1,000 is priced at 100 (known as 'par value') it will cost £1,000 to buy, excluding transaction costs. If it is priced at 95, the £1,000 face value bond will cost £950; if the price is 110, the cost will be £1,100, and so on. If the coupon on the bond is lower than current interest rates then the bond will trade 'below par', and the price will be quoted as less than 100; conversely, if the bond offers a coupon higher than current rates, buyers will have to pay 'above par' – greater than 100 – to persuade the owner to sell.

All sorts of wonderful (and sometimes not so wonderful) variants of this 'classic' bond instrument are available, for example 'equity warrants' may be attached, repayment may be in a different currency from the original loan, the date of repayment may be brought forward under certain circumstances, etc., but the straightforward fixed-rate, medium-term bond is still immensely popular with both borrowers and investors.

An 'equity warrant' is an option giving the right, but not the obligation, to buy shares at a fixed price up to a stated date. We discuss options in Unit 9.

100 Coupon Value.
8%

Exercise 3.1

A corporate bond with a face value of £100 and a coupon rate of 8% matures in two years with a bullet repayment. What is the price of the bond if the yield to maturity is:

(i)   8%?

(ii) 6%?

(iii) 10%?

108   208
1   1
─────   ─────
0.92   0.84
1.08   1.18

274.   100   174

8   108 $\overline{\left(1+r\right)^{n}}$
1.08 1.19

7.41   90.75

BOX 3.2   WHEN IS A EUROBOND NOT A EURO BOND?

At present, most of the time! The term 'euro' as in eurobonds, euromarkets etc. simply means 'international, outside the country of origin' and is not

1.1664

8   108
1.068   1.132

0.94
7.51   95.406
7.521

1.042

1.0638297

8   108
7.213   89.256

linked to Europe directly or the European Union specifically. Thus we have eurodollars and euroyen, but soon not eurodeutschmarks or eurofrenchfrancs when they are replaced by the 'euro' itself.

Unfortunately the potential confusion is unlikely to disappear in the near future, but the meaning will, one hopes, usually be clear from the context – though the idea of domestic euros and euroeuros will take some getting used to.

So what is the difference between a eurobond and a euro bond? A eurobond is a euromarkets bond but not necessarily in euros. A euro bond is in euros but is not necessarily issued in the euromarkets.

3.2 QUANTIFYING INTEREST RATE RISK

In this sub-section we discuss how to quantify and measure interest rate risk. This will provide a framework for the rest of the unit.

First, we need to find some way to identify the exposure to interest risk in a usable way, and preferably to capture and encapsulate it in a single measure. We approach this ideal in two steps: **gap analysis** and **duration**. We then proceed to thinking about what to *do* with our new-found ability to quantify interest risk!

So far we have only identified that we are 'at risk' if interest rates vary. Let us be more precise about this exposure.

Assume we have title to an inward cash flow of £1m in two years' time. What is the worth of this asset? It is the present value, discounted for two years at an appropriate discount rate. For the sake of simplicity, let us assume that this cash flow comes from a debt instrument (e.g. a fixed-rate bond), and therefore that the relevant two-year interest rate would be the appropriate discount rate.

The YTM will change (and hence the value of the bond in the secondary market) following variations of the reference rate, inflation, etc.

BOX 3.3 SPOT RATES

In the preceding paragraph we calmly talk about 'the two-year interest rate'. But what do we mean by this?

Part of the answer to that question lies in the idea of 'basis'. 'Basis' simply means the key factors which define how interest will be calculated. For example, are we talking about fixed or floating rate debt? Is it for secured or unsecured debt, is it for a 'bullet' loan or an 'amortising' one ('bullet' simply means the principal is paid in one lump at maturity, 'amortising' that repayment is spread over the life of the loan)? What is the reference rate to be used? Usually one works with a 'benchmark': for fixed rate debt, typically the interest rate for domestic government debt in that currency for the appropriate length of time. For floating rate debt, reference may be made to the interbank rate or to a domestic 'base rate'.

So we have chosen our 'basis', two-year fixed rate British government debt. However, a two-year UK Treasury Note will not only pay out money at maturity but also interest amounts every six months (the 'coupons'). Thus the so-called two-year rate is a blend of rates suitable for six months, one year, eighteen months and two years. Granted, this blend will be heavily weighted towards the end because the final cash flow of principal plus interest is so much larger than the other amounts. Nevertheless, the bald 'two-year rate', or 'yield', seen in newspapers or on dealers' screens is not strictly accurate for our £1m to be received in one 'lump' in two years' time.

What we require is the interest rate from now stretching out to two years *with no intervening cash flows*. This is called the **spot rate** of interest. It turns out that spot rates such as this are useful and important in debt (and other) valuation.

Unfortunately, spot rates are difficult to calculate as a matter of course without sophisticated – and fast – computer methods. Doing so is beyond the requirements of B821. When we need such rates, we will just assume that they have been calculated for us, or will use simple examples that are amenable to straightforward solution.

Do not confuse the spot rate of interest with the 'spot exchange rate' that you will meet in Unit 8, which is simply the exchange rate for delivery in usually two working days.

Noting the information in Box 3.3, let us assume that the two-year spot rate is currently 6% per annum. The worth of our right to receive £1m in two years' time is thus:

$$£1m / (1 + 0.06)^2 = £889,996.44$$

But what will happen to the value if the two-year spot rate rises by, say, 1%? The asset will now be worth:

$$£1m / (1 + 0.07)^2 = £873,438.73$$

a fall (or loss) of about 1.86%.

Of course, if interest rates had *fallen* by 1%, we would have made a profit of similar magnitude.

We can generalise this idea by saying that:

> interest rate risk is the change in PV of a set of cash flows for a given change in the relevant interest rate(s).

This is the quantified version of our basic definition of interest rate risk. Now that we at least know what we are talking about, it is time to begin considering how to measure in a practical and systematic way the exposure to this form of risk.

SUMMARY

In this short section we have defined carefully what is meant by interest rate risk. Initially, we described it qualitatively as the gain or loss sustained as interest rates change.

Later you were able to quantify this definition as the change in the present value of the cash flows for a particular change in interest rates. In the middle of the section we recapped on what is meant by a 'bond', an instrument you met first in Unit 1. We also investigated the idea of spot rates, a subject we will meet again later in this unit.

4 GAP ANALYSIS

In Section 3, we defined what we mean by interest rate risk. We discussed it in the simple case of an asset consisting of a single cash flow and then generalised to 'a set of cash flows'. The implication was of a set of inward (positive) cash flows, but it could equally well be a sequence of outward (negative) flows. This latter situation could be regarded as valuing the cost of a liability, for example the flows associated with paying the interest and principal amounts of a loan.

4.1   THE CONCEPT OF GAP ANALYSIS

What is our exposure if we have *both* an asset of a £1m receipt and a liability to pay £400,000, each in two years' time?

At 6%, the asset value is £889,996.44 as before; the liability is worth:

$$-£400k / (1 + 0.06)^2 = -£355,998.58$$

These figures become £873,438.73 and £349,375.49 if rates rise to 7%. So our net change in value is:

$$= (£873,438.73 - £889,996.44) - (£349,375.49 - £355,998.58)$$

$$= -£16,557.71 + £6,623.09$$

$$= -£9,934.62$$

It is unlikely to surprise you that we achieve the same result if we *net off* the asset and liability amounts before discounting, but the point is an important one. It shows that we can treat all positive and negative cash flows as a *portfolio,* and as long as we are careful to allocate each cash flow to its appropriate time-slot, our exposure is directly related to the absolute amount of the net cash flow for each period. It is the absolute amount, i.e. without reference to whether it is positive or negative, which is important because interest risk can be caused by any net surplus or shortage; if there is a surplus, we could lose money if interest rates decrease, and vice versa for a shortage. There is some natural reduction in overall risk if surpluses in some periods are 'matched' by shortages in others; for example if an organisation had a surplus of £5m for two months it would be more exposed to interest rate changes than if it had a £5m surplus for one month followed by a £5m shortage for the second month. In the first case, if interest rates fell by 1%, it would lose £5m $\times$ $0.01 \times {}^2/_{12}$, but in the second situation it would lose 1% for the first month and gain about the same in terms of lower borrowing costs for the shortage period. Nevertheless, risk is produced by shortages *or* surpluses, so both need to be monitored carefully.

The technique for monitoring this risk is called gap analysis – we provide ourselves with a table which shows our portfolio of cash surpluses and shortfalls over time. An example of a typical gap-chart table is shown in Figure 4.1. The larger the 'gap' in any period, the greater contribution to our overall interest risk. With a spread-sheet, quantifying the actual value change for a given change in rates can be done almost automatically.

TOD= today;
TOM= tomorrow.

Currency: _____   Date: _____

	Tod	Tom	Spot	3d	4d	1 wk	2 wk	3 wk	1 mth	2 mth	3 mth	4 mth	5 mth	6 mth	9 mth	1 yr	2 yr	3 yr	4 yr	5 yr	> 5 yr
Opening +																					
Inflow																						
Net +																						
Opening −																						
Outflow																						
Net −																						
Net																						
Cum net																						

Figure 4.1   A generic gap chart

So a gap chart is somewhat similar in design to the familiar DCF layout, except that we do not actually calculate the NPV. The difference between gap charts and DCF tables is typically in terms of the fineness of our gradations, and that we track inflows and outflows separately. For example, when producing a DCF table for, say, an investment appraisal, one may well just divide the timescale into whole years, treating everything from day 1 to day 365 in year n as happening at the end of the period. A fairly coarse sieve, but sufficient for the purpose.

For gap analysis one is likely to be a little more discriminating, particularly in the 'near' time periods. It would not be unusual to see a gap chart where the flows for the next month were tracked on a day-by-day basis, those for the following two months divided on a weekly schedule, then monthly out to two or three years. After that a 'coarse' chart of quarters, half-years or whole years might prevail.

Who in an organisation should maintain the gap chart? Whichever department or individual is responsible for monitoring cash movements and/or ensuring enough money is in the right place at the right time. In a large organisation this might be a joint responsibility of a whole treasury team. In a more modest firm it may be part of the job of one manager. But it will be somebody's task whatever the scale of the business – and the tools and the principles are the same regardless of size or sector.

The company's accounting information system will probably keep track of the exact dates for each flow; with luck, if the system allows, the data can be captured for the gap chart directly and automatically from the accounts database. Whether the input is automatic or manual, the point of the gap chart is to present the manager with helpful information about the future pattern of cash flows. For example, this might be used in discussion with the organisation's bankers when negotiating short-term borrowing needs.

Bearing in mind that the gap chart is a way of summarising data, it is important to be realistic about maintaining its usability. It is a trade-off between accuracy of information and risk of destroying functionality with proliferating columns. In Figure 4.1 the number of columns and the periods they represent are only examples. The key point is that the grid presents an overview of the cash inflows and outflows showing at what times the organisation is predicted to have significant excess or shortage of funds. The third column is labelled 'spot' simply because many transactions in the financial markets are traded for delivery in two working days, which is called 'spot delivery'. Thus, if you were placing funds on deposit with a bank for three months, it would be usual for the cash to be handed over in two days, and it to be returned (with interest) in three months and two days. If deals with a start date other than spot are required, e.g. beginning from today, then this should be made clear so that there is no confusion between the two parties as to when to expect settlement.

With computer spreadsheets it is easy and useful to summarise gap information visually by displaying the gap chart as a graph, which gives an immediate impression of when the business is expecting major shortages or surpluses. A graphical representation loses some detail, so this form is most commonly seen as a day-end summary, often then passed on as part of the report to management. At the end of this sub-section we will look at a worked example, and there you will be able to see both forms of presentation.

It is implicit in what we have said so far that we are considering the cash flows within a single currency. Organisations conducting significant business in numerous currencies are likely to maintain a gap chart and undertake gap management in each of the currencies with which they are concerned.

BOX 4.1   INTEREST RATE RISK AND FOREIGN EXCHANGE RISK – A GAP VIEW

In Unit 8 you will study the risks associated with foreign exchange and their management. There you will see one connection between foreign exchange and interest rates, namely that the difference between spot and forward exchange rates is predicated upon the relevant interest rates in the two currencies. Take that link as true for now – Unit 8 will prove it – and let us see here that 'multi-currency gap analysis' shows another link between interest and forex risk management.

Let us consider a company that has significant cash flows in sterling and dollars. It, therefore, maintains a two-dimensional gap chart for each currency.

What would it tell the company's cash managers if they stacked the gap charts, in effect producing a 3-d bi-currency gap chart (see Figure 4.2)? This would become a multi- rather than bi-currency chart as the business started using other currencies.

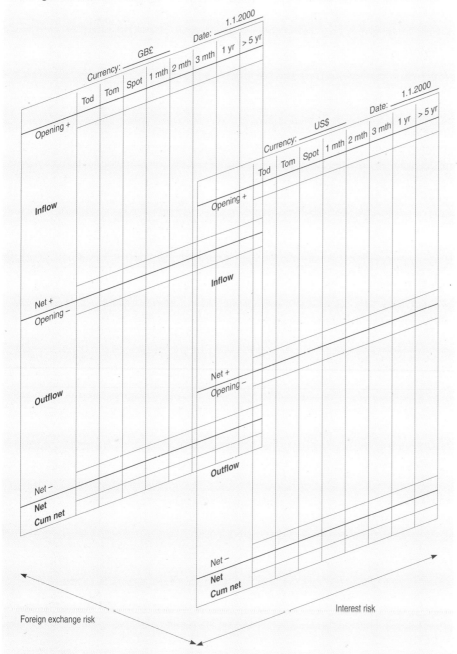

Figure 4.2   Conceptual bi-currency gap chart

Consider how the charts would look if the business was a start-up and only had a pair of cash flows to worry about: a receipt of US$1.6m and a payment of £1m, both in two months' time. A condensed version of the two gap charts is shown in Figure 4.3.

The sterling chart would show a net deficit of £1m, and the dollar chart a net surplus of US$1.6m. But by looking 'through' the 3-d chart – in essence, along the y-axis rather than the x-axis – we can see that in fact the overall effect on cash flow for both currencies could be due to just one transaction, namely selling sterling for US dollars with delivery in two months' time. This could be sorted out with just one hedging transaction, rather than having to deal with each currency separately. (The details of hedging with forward foreign exchange will be discussed in Unit 8.)

Generalising, we can use a 3-d gap chart to monitor both interest rate risk *and* foreign exchange risk. We merely change our point of view when looking at the 'gap cube'.

Currency: GB£   Date: 1.1.2000

	Tod	Tom	Spot	1 mth	2 mth	3 mth	1 yr	> 5 yr
Opening +								
Inflow								
Net +								
Opening −					−1m			
Outflow								
Net −					−1m			
Net					−1m			
Cum net					−1m	−1m	−1m	−1m

Currency: US$ Date: 1.1.2000

	Tod	Tom	Spot	1 mth	2 mth	3 mth	1 yr	> 5 yr
Opening +					1.6m			
Inflow								
Net +					1.6m			
Opening −								
Outflow								
Net −								
Net					1.6m			
Cum net					1.6m	1.6m	1.6m	1.6m

Figure 4.3 Bi-currency gap chart with transaction

You do not need to become a technical expert in multi-currency gap analysis, but it *is* helpful to understand the simple process underlying this very useful monitoring method, and to see the way that forex and interest risk can – and should – be managed together. By considering exchange *and* timing risks at the same time you can often sort out both with the same ameliorating transaction.

Having got your gap chart (or cube), what do you do with it? The most common use is for cash management. It provides 'early warning' of forthcoming cash shortages, and how long the deficits are predicted to last. This enables managers to make appropriate provision in good time. It also alerts managers to excessive interest exposure because of large net in- or outflows in particular periods, again enabling risk control action. This is as important for a public-sector or NFP organisation as for a private-sector one; *all* organisations, of whatever type, should track their cash flows with equal care, accuracy and precision.

We will discuss later in this unit some of the financial products available for managing the risk associated with such cash flow imbalances, but the starting point must be an information system to instruct the decision-making process.

4.2 GAP ANALYSIS: A WORKED EXAMPLE

To finish this discussion of the simple but very useful gap analysis technique, let us look at a worked example, seeing how various forms of transaction will impinge upon a gap chart.

Example: SoftKing Trust, gap chart for 18 June 1999

SoftKing is a not-for-profit enterprise which provides general practice and minor surgical services; it is basically a European equivalent of an American 'health management organisation', i.e. providing more services than a typical doctors' group practice but fewer than a small hospital.

A number of transactions are reported to the treasurer by various parts of the organisation; these represent both operational and capital cash flows. In reality, figures caused by operations are much more common than capital transactions, but let us assume that for SoftKing today is an unusual day when a major capital investment is agreed. This enables us to see the gap chart effect of all transaction types.

Figure 4.4 shows the 'opening position' brought forward from the previous day. The second shows the first part of the day's transactions included; you are then asked to complete the chart as an Exercise, so the position including all the day's transactions is shown at the end of the

Currency: £000   Date: 18.6.99

	Tod	Tom	Spot	3d	4d	1 wk	2 wk	3 wk	1 mth	2 mth	3 mth	4 mth	5 mth	6 mth	9 mth	1 yr	2 yr	3 yr	4 yr	5 yr	> 5 yr
Opening +	5					15	6			22	7			53	19	47					
Inflow																					
Net +	5					15	6			22	7			53	19	47					
Opening −		−7					−10	−17			−45	−21									
Outflow																					
Net −		−7					−10	−17			−45	−21									
Net	5	−7				15	6	−10	−17	22	7	−45	−21	53	19	47					
Cum net	5	−2	−2	−2	−2	13	19	9	−8	14	21	−24	−45	8	27	74	74	74	74	74	74

Figure 4.4 SoftKing Trust opening position

Unit in the Answers to Exercises. Remember that gap analysis is only an information system; we will return to the example to deal with the resulting gaps once we have covered the interest risk management techniques needed so to do.

The following transactions are reported to the funds manager:

- medical and other supplies are delivered, the invoice for £35,000 is payable in 30 days
- salaries of £85,000 are payable on 25/6/99
- service invoices totalling £20,000 are issued, payment due in 30 days
- utility bills (power, water, telephone, etc.) totalling £5,000 are received, payable in two weeks.

These cash flows are included in the gap chart shown in Figure 4.5.

Currency: £000   Date: 18.6.99

	Tod	Tom	Spot	3d	4d	1 wk	2 wk	3 wk	1 mth	2 mth	3 mth	4 mth	5 mth	6 mth	9 mth	1 yr	2 yr	3 yr	4 yr	5 yr	> 5 yr
Opening +	5					15	6			22	7 32			53 78	19 44	47 72					
									20												
Inflow																					
Net +	5					15	6		20	22	7			53	19	47					
Opening −		−7	200						−10	−17	−540	−45	−21	−100 200							
						−85	−5		−35					−1040							
Outflow																					
Net −		−7				−85	−5	−10	−52			−45	−21								
Net	5	−7				−70	1	−10	−32	22	7	−45	−21	53	19	47					
Cum net	5	−2	−2	−2	−2	−72	−71	−81	−113	−91	−84	−129	−150	−97	−78	−31	−31	−31	−31	−31	−31

Figure 4.5   SoftKing Trust, including first set of transactions

Exercise 4.1 _____

Post the following transactions to the SoftKing gap chart as shown in Figure 4.5.

- A one-year service contract for £100,000 has been signed, payment to be received in four equal amounts in 3, 6, 9 and 12 months' time
- The contract for building a new clinic is signed. It involves the following payments:

Purchase of land	£200,000	2 days from today
Stage payment 1	£500,000	3 months
Stage payment 2	£1,000,000	6 months
Completion payment	£600,000	12 months
Equipment	£440,000	12 months

SUMMARY

This section has been concerned with a simple but powerful technique for converting data about an organisation's cash flows into information for management. The intention is to assist in the control of two types of financial risk: interest rate and cash flow risks.

We have seen how it provides information for managing the former; the latter is even more straightforward, in that the method automatically provides warning of when cash shortages are forecast. Thus funds or borrowing capacity can be provided at the right time.

Incidentally, the spread of personal computers makes the practical use of the system much more flexible. A simple spreadsheet can be constructed to hold the data, as shown in our examples. The key benefit a computer provides is that the *output* can be rapidly tailored to present the information in the most appropriate way, taking into account not only the intended user (e.g. graphic summary for senior management, details for the funds manager) but also the data itself (e.g. shrinking empty columns, expanding ones with cash flows). Also, as long as the input is done accurately, errors will not creep in at later stages. Indeed, if the organisation has an integrated computer network much of the data can be captured direct from the relevant area without requiring extra work with a separate reporting system.

We hope we have emphasised that this information process is important whatever the nature of the organisation. It does not matter whether it be from the private, public or NFP sector; every enterprise involves funds flowing in and out – and needs to track all these flows. Similarly, it is just as important for a small firm to manage its flows as it is for a giant multinational; mistakes of hundreds of pounds may be more dangerous for a small organisation than hundreds of *thousands* would be for a large one.

5 DURATION

The gap analysis system gives a useful overview of the risks facing a business (or part of a business such as a department or subsidiary) but it is less helpful when considering the value of an individual asset or liability, since it is fundamentally a summary method. Also it is of little help when, for example, you are trying to make a comparison between investments in competing assets – a pair of eurobonds, say. For this we need an actual *measure* with which we can say Choice A is more/less exposed to movements in interest rates than Choice B. For this we need to investigate the concept of duration.

The idea was invented by Professor F. R. Macaulay who, in a book he wrote in 1938, introduced the term 'duration' (also known as **Macaulay duration**). An important further step was taken by F. M. Reddington in the 1950s, when he used duration to develop **immunisation** strategies.

5.1 SO WHAT IS WRONG WITH 'MATURITY'?

An important question which we need to answer is: why go to the trouble of calculating this duration measure? Why not just use maturity – which is usually a lot easier to ascertain – to compare two bonds, or to estimate their exposure to interest rate movements?

The simple answer to this is that maturity is some guide to interest rate exposure, but is by no means sufficient or complete. Let us use an example to see this:

> We are trying to compare two bonds, A and B. Both instruments will mature in five years; A pays a coupon of 3%, B pays a coupon of 10%. They are both issued by the same borrower (thus having identical credit risk characteristics) and have a yield to maturity of 7%. Note that, as we are considering buying one of them at today's market price, the YTM – which is just the IRR, remember – will equal the market's current demand for investment return for this borrower. In other words, 7% is the current 'fair' return.

See Exercise 3.1 to remind yourself how to calculate the price of a bond as the YTM varies.

> Let us have a look at the way the two bonds change in value as the required yield rises or falls from the current 7%. Remember that the value of a bond is simply the PV of the stream of cash flows it represents. Of course, while the *yields* are the same in each case, since B actually pays out a lot more cash than A, the *prices* of the two bonds will be very different. So we are really concerned about the percentage change in each price as rates change.

The values for a bond with a face value of £100 are shown in Table 5.1.

[handwritten: 3%]   *[handwritten: 10% coupon yield]*

Table 5.1	Comparison of bonds A and B for different YTMs			
YTM %	Price of A	Change %	Price of B	Change %
3	100.00	+19.62	132.06	+17.59
5	91.34	+9.26	121.65	+8.32
7	83.60	0	112.30	0
10	73.46	−12.12	100.00	−10.95

Remember, bond arithmetic is just NPV/DCF stuff with different labels on the terms of the equation.

[handwritten calculation notes:]
1 2 3 4 5
100   3   3   3   3   103
0.95 0.90 1.36 0.82 0.78
2.85 27 2.58
2.46
80.34
90.93.

Notice that when the required YTM for the bond equals the coupon rate, then it is valued at its face value of £100. Even if the face value of the bond is not £100 it is conventional to value bonds in 'lumps' of 100.

Notice also that the coupon rate was fixed at the time of issue. Depending on subsequent changes in market interest rates or the credit standing of the issuer, the value of the bond will move in the secondary market to remain 'fair' (see column YTM%), that is, the market will require a higher or lower return than the initially fixed coupon rate. So, the value of the bond in the secondary market will fluctuate above or below the original issue price (see Change %).

We can see that bond A is more susceptible to changes in interest rates than bond B, even though they are for the same maturity. We can straight away conclude that maturity alone is not a good enough measure to tell us what we need to know.

It is worth noting that for both bonds, value *falls* as interest rates, and hence yields to maturity, *rise*. This follows directly from the definition of bond value as being the NPV of the cash flows. In any DCF calculation the PV tends towards zero as the discount rate rises. For bonds, since all the cash flows are positive from the viewpoint of the owner, this becomes 'PV *falls* as discount rate *rises*'.

What is different between the two bonds? They have the same credit quality, the same YTM and the same maturity *but differing cash flow sequences*. It is obvious, therefore, that our measure must take into account the cash flows of our instrument *and* their timings, combining them neatly into a single number. Duration does this for us.

BOX 5.1 IMMUNISATION AGAINST INTEREST RATE CHILLS

The concept of duration was first applied to the assets and liabilities of life insurance companies. If such a company is large enough, its liabilities – that is the life insurance repayments it will have to pay out – are predictable with a high degree of accuracy. To remain solvent, the life insurance company has to ensure that the premiums (after expenses and profit) are invested in assets (in practice often low-risk, predictable instruments such as bonds) which have the same present value as that of the liabilities. But will the two sets still match when interest rates change?

If bonds could be purchased which had exactly the same maturities as the liabilities (and paid no intermediate coupons which would need to be reinvested at uncertain future interest rates), the life insurance company would have no difficulty in meeting its liabilities since each bond could be held to maturity when it would pay off a known amount. However, in real life, only bonds of certain particular maturities are available, and they *do* pay coupons. Reddington suggested that if:

- the present value of the assets is equal to that of the liabilities

and

- the *duration* of the assets is equal to that of the liabilities

then the portfolio would be *immunised*. This means that the PV of the assets would continue to match that of the liabilities *even if interest rates changed*. In other words, the assets would provide sufficient funds to meet the liabilities irrespective of movements in interest rates.

In other words, the insurance company would have removed its exposure to interest rate risk by ensuring that the overall value of its assets always matched that of its liabilities even as rates changed. The important point to note is that this would be true even though the individual cash flows and timings differed dramatically between the constituent assets and liabilities, a very worthwhile reduction in exposure.

How this works you will see shortly, but it is worth keeping in mind this practical use of the seemingly esoteric idea of duration. The concept of immunising a sequence of cash flows can and is applied much more widely than just to managing life insurance portfolios.

Immunisation is a dynamic concept because duration changes as interest rates vary and/or time to maturity shortens.

In the example in Box 5.1 of the use of duration, it was implied that insurance companies invested mainly in debt instruments such as government or corporate bonds. While they do invest in such a manner to a significant extent, they also have huge amounts of other asset types, such as equities, property, etc., in their portfolios. Provided you can make reasonable predictions about the future cash flows expected to be generated by such assets – for example, the dividends for equities, the rentals for property – *you can make use of the duration and immunisation ideas*. However, it is easier to understand the techniques if we discuss them in terms of fixed-rate bonds, because such instruments have a neat, easy-to-describe cash flow sequence.

For example, if we talked about 'an IBM US$ 5% 2015 bond', the set of cash flows is completely defined: for every $1,000 face value, IBM will pay interest every year of $50, and also repay the $1,000 principal at maturity in 2015. Because of this simplicity and clarity, we will proceed by discussing duration in terms of bond investment alone – but never forget that the technique can be applied to *any* known (or predicted) series of cash flows.

5.2   A MEASURE THAT WORKS

Duration, in simple language, is an average measure of the time you have to wait to receive the cash flows from a bond. Let us take three examples;

1   A four-year bond which has a zero coupon rate.

0	1	2	3	4
–	–	–	–	100

All the cash flow arises in year 4. Therefore, the duration must be in four years.

2   A four-year bond which has a 5% coupon rate.

0	1	2	3	4
–	5	5	5	105

The average time we have to wait to get our cash flow is less than four years, as part of the cash flow is received in years 1–3.

3   A four-year bond which has a 20% coupon rate.

0	1	2	3	4
–	20	20	20	120

The average time we have to wait to get our cash flow is much less than four years, as a significant amount of the cash flow is received in years 1–3.

To be able to calculate the average time, or duration, precisely we need to look at the mathematics behind it.

Duration is actually a **weighted average maturity**, where the weighting for each time period is the PV of the cash flow occurring in that time-slot. By using the PVs of the relevant cash flows as the weighting for each time period, t_i, we ensure that the overall measure correctly reflects the relative importance of each t in the overall result. The equation may, at first glance, look horrible but is simply condensing into figures the idea of a weighted average maturity.

$$D = \frac{1}{P} \times \left(t_1 \times \frac{CF_1}{(1+r)^{t_1}} + t_2 \times \frac{CF_2}{(1+r)^{t_2}} + \ldots t_n \times \frac{CF_n}{(1+r)^{t_n}} \right)$$

where

$$D = \frac{1}{P} \times \left(t_1 \, \frac{CF_i}{(1+r)^{t_i}} + \right) \ldots$$

D   = duration

P   = price of the bond

t_i = time of receipt (or payment) of CF_i

CF_i = cash flow taking place at time t_i

r = discount rate

To see that this equation really does represent a true weighted average, note that the definition of the price, P, is the sum of $PV(CF)_i$. Since we are dividing all the terms by P, the equation is of the form:

Weighted average is discussed in Section 3.2.7 of *Vital Statistics*.

$$D = t_i \times \frac{w_1}{P} + t_2 \times \frac{w_2}{P} + \ldots + t_n \times \frac{w_n}{P}$$

where each term $\dfrac{CF_i}{(1+r)^{t_i}}$ has been represented by w_i

and $P = w_i + w_2 + \ldots + w_n$.

This is the normal form for a weighted average.

You may find it easier to understand the formula if you look at it with $t_1, t_2 \ldots t_n$ replaced by $1, 2 \ldots n$. In other words, with the cash flows taking place exact numbers of years in the future. But never forget that, in reality, t can represent any length of time – the DCF equation doesn't mind and neither should you! For example, if you are dealing with bonds or their equivalents, the periods are only whole numbers of years 1 day out of 365. In other words, on a coupon payment day it is exactly 1 year until the next interest payment, but for every other day it will be only a fractional part of a year to the next cash flow. Thus, as an example, two months after the last interest payment it will be $^{10}/_{12}$ of a year to the next coupon date, $1^{10}/_{12}$ years to the one after that, and so on.

The durations for Bonds A and B from Section 5.1 are calculated in Table 5.2.

Table 5.2	Durations of bonds A and B			
Time	**CF$_A$**	**PV(CF$_A$)**	***t* × PV(CF$_A$)**	
1	3	2.804	2.804	
2	3	2.620	5.241	
3	3	2.449	7.347	
4	3	2.289	9.155	
5	103	73.438	367.188	
		83.599	391.734	Duration A **4.69** years
Time	**CF$_B$**	**PV(CF$_B$)**	***t* × PV(CF$_B$)**	
1	10	9.346	9.346	
2	10	8.734	17.469	
3	10	8.163	24.489	
4	10	7.629	30.516	
5	110	78.428	392.142	
		112.301	473.962	Duration B **4.22** years

r = 7% for duration calculation (i.e. the yield to maturity)

We can see that there is now a difference between the two bonds, and A (which is more volatile with respect to interest rates) has a longer duration than B. So our new measure is an improvement over just looking at the maturity, inasmuch as it distinguishes between instruments with the same maturity but different exposure to interest rate changes.

Exercise 5.1

Calculate the duration of the three bonds introduced at the start of this section.

(i)   Four-year zero-coupon bond

(ii) Four-year 5% coupon bond

(iii) Four-year 20% coupon bond

The YTM is 10% and each bond has a face value of £100.

BOX 5.2   MATURITY WRONG, DURATION RIGHT

In fact, we can show that sometimes maturity 'points' the wrong way, but duration always shows which bond is more exposed to interest rate movements.

Let us compare bond A with a new alternative, bond C. Again, it has the same issuer but this time it has six years to maturity and pays a coupon of 15%.

Looking at the maturity, we would assume C was more volatile with respect to interest rates. In fact, as can be seen from Table 5.3 below, C is a little bit *less* susceptible to rate changes than is A. Oops!

Table 5.3 Comparison of bonds A and C

YTM %	Price of A £	Change %	Price of C £	Change %
3	100	+19.62	165.01	+19.46
5	91.34	+9.26	150.76	+9.14
7	83.60	0	138.13	0
9	76.66	−8.30	126.92	−8.12
10	73.46	−12.12	121.78	−11.84

So what about the duration of C? At 7% YTM, it is **4.60 years**, which is indeed slightly shorter than A at **4.69 years**.

In general we can say:

(i) The *longer* the duration, the *higher* the exposure to interest rate risk.

and

(ii) *Any* sequence of cash flows with a duration of *n* years will have exactly the same volatility with respect to interest rates as any *other* sequence with an equal duration of *n* years.

This is very important as it means that we can indeed use duration as a meaningful way to compare streams of cash flows. And remember that, although we have worked with bonds for clarity and convenience, the system works for any set of cash flows, whatever asset or liability they are derived from.

> Duration is, ultimately, a measure of how sensitive the present value of a series of cashflows is to a small change in the discount rate. See Section 5.3.

Why does this work? Because with duration each cash flow is properly represented and given due weight in the calculation. Maturity, on the other hand, simply looks at the final amount – which is not a sufficiently accurate method.

The workings of compound interest mean that a cash flow of a given size, say £1,000, will be more exposed to interest rate changes the further in the future is its payment date. This is simply saying that interest rates have more time to work their evil way (or benign, if rates are falling!) with the value of a flow a long time in the future than on one due for payment shortly. Table 5.4 shows the change in PV(£1,000) for different interest rates for payment in 1, 5 and 10 years:

Table 5.4 Different rates, different maturities (£1,000)

Rate	1yr	5yrs	10yrs
5%	£952.38	£783.53	£613.91
10%	£909.09	£620.92	£385.54
15%	£869.57	£497.18	£247.18

For the 1 year column, the PV at 15% is 91.30% of the PV at 5%; the equivalent figure for 10 years is 40.26%, which confirms the point about increased volatility overtime.

Because the weighting system used in duration uses the PVs of the cash flows, the relative importance of each item is properly reflected. So duration gives us a proper, workable measure.

BOX 5.3   ZERO-COUPON BONDS

Since the last cash flow for a bond includes the principal payment, this cash flow item will dominate the calculation and make the duration less than, but reasonably close to, the maturity of the bond for shorter maturity bonds.

For long-lived bonds paying coupons, the difference between maturity and duration can become surprisingly big. The US Treasury 'long bond' has a 30-year maturity, but at normal interest rates its duration is only around 15 to 18 years – little more than half. What is happening is that, while the final principal repayment is still 10 or 20 times larger than any one of the yearly interest flows, all those coupon payments (30 of them) mean that the relative importance of the final cash flow is lessened.

But investors with long-lived liabilities (e.g. pension funds, life insurance companies) need assets which are equivalently long-lived.

The duration of a bond can never exceed its maturity, but what kind of instrument will have the longest possible duration?

We can see from the earlier examples that the smaller the coupon, the longer the duration. The final payment becomes relatively more important the smaller the intervening cash flows. The ultimate version of this is where the bond pays *no* coupons, just a lump sum at maturity.

These are – quite logically – called **zero-coupon bonds**, usually abbreviated to 'zeroes'. And they are the only type of bond where the duration is equal to the maturity. So a 30-year zero-coupon bond is *really* a long-lived asset.

This may seem to be of interest only to pension fund managers, but think back to Box 3.3 concerning **spot rates**. What we had there was the need to find an interest rate which was correct for a single cash flow at a particular future time, with no intervening muddle.

That is exactly what we see with zero-coupon bonds. Indeed, what we refer to as a **spot interest rate** would typically be called the zero-coupon rate by a financier. Same thing, different label. We will meet these terms again when looking at 'swaps'.

Activity 5.1 ─────────────────────────────────

Try to estimate what the duration of a 'century bond' (one with a 100-year maturity date) would be. Let it have a 5% coupon, and a 5% yield to maturity. Either use your spreadsheet to calculate the answer (if you use the Fill right function of Excel it is surprisingly quick and simple to do) or try to guess a 'ballpark' answer if your PC is not nearby.

My spreadsheet gives a duration result just short of 21 years. Quite a difference from a maturity of 100 years! Incidentally, this is not a completely silly example. The Disney Corporation actually issued a 'century bond' in 1996.

5.3   DURATION AND QUANTIFYING INTEREST EXPOSURE

The duration formula we have seen so far provides us with a good measure with which we can compare portfolios of cash flows. The criterion is simple: the longer the duration, the greater the interest exposure.

But we can use another version of the duration formula derived directly from the PV equation, which will give us even more information, namely an estimate of the amount a portfolio will change in value for a given change in interest rates. This is clearly useful. The relevant formula is:

$$\Delta P = -D \times P \times \frac{1}{(1 + r)} \times \Delta r$$

where:

ΔP = change in price (or value)

D = duration

P = price

r = interest rate

Δr = change in interest rate

Note that as interest rates *rise*, bond prices *fall*.

Alternatively, if we want the percentage change in price, as was calculated in Table 5.1, then the formula is even more convenient as it does not depend upon the current price (though it is needed to calculate D):

$$\frac{\Delta P}{P} \{\text{in } \%\} = -D \times \frac{1}{(1 + r)} \times \Delta r \times 100$$

So, for example, if we take bond A from Table 5.2 we know that with a YTM of 7% it has a price of £100 and a duration of 4.69 years. The effect of a 1% rise in interest rates on the price of the bond would be:

$$\frac{\Delta P}{P} = -4.69 \times \frac{1}{1 + 0.07} \times 0.01 \times 100$$

$$\frac{\Delta P}{P} = -4.38$$

In other words, the price of the bond would fall by £4.38 to £(100 − 4.38) = £95.62.

Exercise 5.2 _____

Calculate the change in price of a bond for a 1% fall in interest rates if the bond has a yield to maturity of 10%, a price of £100.00, and a duration of three years.

_____

BOX 5.4   WHAT DOES THE EQUATION *MEAN*?

So we have a formula picked out of thin air which 'magically' relates the value change to duration and interest rates. Does it represent anything realistic? Actually, it does.

If we drew a graph of value against interest rate (i.e. value plotted up the y-axis and interest rate along the x-axis), what would we be showing? The result of the price equation for each rate of interest. The result would look something like Figure 5.1.

This graphical idea is also discussed in Section 5.4.3 of *Vital Statistics*, where it is also continued into the idea of convexity.

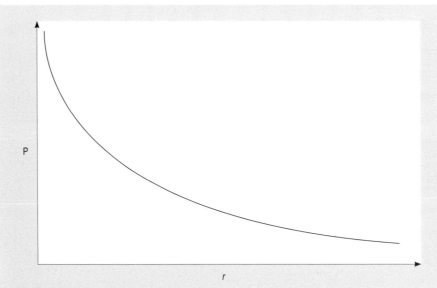

Figure 5.1

For a small change in r (i.e. Δr), we can approximate the curve by a straight line tangential to the curve at (r, P). So the equivalent ΔP will be given by:

ΔP = (gradient of straight line) $\times \Delta r$ (See Figure 5.2)

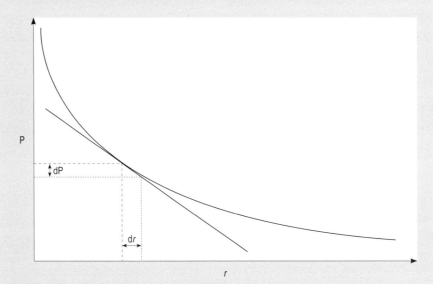

Figure 5.2

This gives us the formula

$$\Delta P = \frac{D \times P \times 1 \times \Delta r}{1 + r} \quad \text{as quoted.}$$

The mathematical derivation of the equation is not required for B821, as long as you understand the graph idea it comes from. For those who prefer to see the algebra, it is shown below. *You do not have to remember it!*

The gradient of the line is given by the first derivative of the PV equation, so:

$$P = \frac{CF_1}{(1 + r)^{t_1}} + \frac{CF_2}{(1 + r)^{t_2}} + \ldots + \frac{CF_n}{(1 + r)^{t_n}}$$

$$\Rightarrow \frac{dP}{dr} = -t_1 \times \frac{CF_1}{(1 + r)^{(t_1 + 1)}} - t_2 \times \frac{CF_2}{(1 + r)^{(t_2 + 1)}} - \ldots t_n \times \frac{CF_n}{(1 + r)^{(t_n + 1)}}$$

$$\Rightarrow \frac{dP}{dr} = \frac{-1}{(1 + r)} \times \left(t_1 \times \frac{CF_1}{(1 + r)^{t_1}} + t_2 \times \frac{CF_2}{(1 + r)^{t_2}} + \ldots t_n \times \frac{CF_n}{(1 + r)^{t_n}} \right)$$

$$\Rightarrow \frac{dP}{dr} = \frac{-1}{(1+r)} \times D \times P$$

$$\Rightarrow \Delta P = -D \times P \times \frac{1}{1+r} \times \Delta r$$

So now we know it *does* come from something sensible, we can use the formula without worrying further about its origin.

You should have noted from the material in Box 5.4 that we are using a straight line *approximation* to the value curve, and so can only apply it for fairly small changes in interest rates. We could then 're-base' our calculation (i.e. recalculate the gradient) for further changes in rates.

This is true for the duration measure and immunisation tactic as well. If you have immunised your liabilities with an asset portfolio of equal duration, then the practical protection is very good for changes up to about +/−1%. In practice this is perfectly adequate, as this would give you time to re-align the assets and liabilities if they had drifted apart. They might not drift, but you cannot be certain without checking the particular sequence of cash flows.

This variation of duration with interest rates should not be over-stated. Table 5.5 shows the duration for bond A at varying interest rates. As you can see, the differences are scarcely dramatic. Duration is a stable enough measure to be useful.

Table 5.5   Duration of bond A at various interest rates

r %	D yrs
1	4.73
5	4.70
10	4.66
15	4.62
20	4.57
30	4.46

5.4 WORKED EXAMPLE

Let us conclude the duration discussion with a worked example, creating a simple asset portfolio that 'immunises' a known future liability.

Risk plc has to pay £100m in exactly 3.5 years' time. Interest rates are currently at 8% p.a. for any maturity of loan. Risk plc wishes to invest now in a way which ensures that it will be able to meet the £100m liability at the appropriate time, and decides to invest in bonds so as to be able to do this.

It chooses two bonds in which to invest. In both cases their next coupons are due in exactly six months.

- Bond A: a four-year 10% coupon bond paying yearly coupons. With a YTM of 8% and maturity 3.5 years away, the current price is 110.81. The duration, calculated in the normal way, is 3.00 years.

- Bond B: a six-year 3% coupon bond paying yearly coupons with maturity 5.5 years away. The current price is 79.90. The duration is 5.01 years.

You can check the figures if you wish by looking at the Excel spreadsheet RISKPLC.XLS on CD-ROM 2.

Since the duration of the future liability is 3.5 years, the mix of bonds that is purchased has to have a duration of 3.5 years as well. If we define a to be the proportion of capital invested in bond A, then:

$$a \times 3.00 + (1 - a) \times 5.01 = 3.5$$

Solving this equation for a:

$$a \times 3.00 + 5.01 - a \times 5.01 = 3.5$$

$$a \times (3.00 - 5.01) + 5.01 = 3.5$$

$$-a \times 2.01 + 5.01 = 3.5$$

$$5.01 = 3.5 + a \times 2.01$$

$$1.51 = a \times 2.01$$

$$\frac{1.51}{2.01} = a$$

$$a = 0.751$$

$$b = (1 - a) = (1 - 0.751) = 0.249$$

This gives the proportion to be invested in bond A as 0.751, with the balance of 0.249 in bond B.

The total investment has to be the present value of £100m in 3.5 years' time discounted at 8% per year.

$$\text{i.e. PV} = £100\text{m}/1.08^{3.5} = £76.387\text{m}$$

Thus the investments are:

Bond A: $0.751 \times 76.387 = $ **£57.367m**

Bond B: $0.249 \times 76.387 = $ **£19.020m**

Finally, we need to work out how many bonds of each type we need to purchase to give the right amount of investment in each. These bonds have a face value of £1,000, and the current prices of A and B are 110.81 and 79.90 respectively. Remember that according to the pricing convention for bonds, those prices mean that a £1,000 face value bond will cost £1,108 and £799 respectively. Thus the holdings should be:

A: $57,367,000/1,108 = $ **51,775 bonds**

B: $19,020,000/799 = $ **23,805 bonds**

To confirm that the immunised portfolio does remove the risk of interest rate movement from Risk's ability to meet the liability, let us see what happens to the value of the liability and portfolio if interest rates change immediately after purchasing the portfolio. This is, of course, the most extreme possibility, so if rates actually vary later on – which is more likely – then we know that this is covered by considering the 'immediate movement' scenario.

Table 5.6	An immunised liability and asset portfolio			
r %	PV (liability) £m	PV (assets) £m	PV (assets) – PV (liability) £000	% 'error'
1	96.577	97.001	424	0.437
3	90.172	90.376	204	0.226
5	84.302	84.375	73	0.087
7	78.914	78.927	13	0.016
8	76.387	76.387	0	0.000
9	73.962	73.969	7	0.009
10	71.635	71.656	21	0.029
15	61.314	61.531	217	0.353
20	52.828	53.368	540	1.012

Again, you can check the figures from the spreadsheet if you so choose.

Looking at Table 5.6, this is quite an impressive result. For a change in interest rates of 12% (from 8% to 20%), the portfolio has drifted away from the liability value by just 1%. In practice, Risk plc would have been able to adjust the portfolio well before rates moved so much. More representative would be that, for a +/−1% shift, the drift in this £76,000,000 portfolio would be between £5,000 and £10,000.

SUMMARY

Duration is a measure that has been known for a long time – Macaulay introduced it in the 1930s and Reddington used it in the 1950s – but it became a widely usable technique when personal computers reached the manager's desk. If you can create a DCF spreadsheet for NPV or IRR, you can make it calculate duration at the same time; it effectively just requires adding one more row or column to multiply each PV(cash flow) by the time at which the flow occurs.

Duration gives us a measure that accurately reflects a portfolio of cash flows' exposure to movements in interest rates, unlike maturity which is an insufficient discriminator. Indeed, maturity can actually imply that 'A' is more exposed to interest rate movement than 'B' when in reality it is the other way round. Duration never suffers from this problem, and can even be used to give the actual amount by which a bond or portfolio will change in value for a given change in interest rates.

The measure is not perfect, because at core it is approximating the curve of 'portfolio value' versus 'interest rates' with a straight line. Thus the model is only accurate for reasonably small movements in interest rates; in practice, duration is typically good enough for a rise or fall of one or two percentage points in interest rates. In nearly all cases this is sufficient protection to enable time for managers to take corrective action.

Lastly, remember that, as said in the section and this summary, the systems of duration and immunisation can be applied to *any* known sequence of cash flows. It is most often used for debt instruments such as fixed-rate bonds, but the system's applicability is not confined to such a restricted use.

6 INTEREST RISK MANAGEMENT INSTRUMENTS: FRAs AND FUTURES

Now that we are able to measure interest risk properly, it is time to look at some of the products available to help managers control it.

As we have seen in the discussion about duration and immunisation, sometimes we can take care of interest risk simply by judicious choice of the assets and liabilities we take on.

For example, if we need to raise debt finance to proceed with a project, by ensuring that the duration of the 'debt portfolio' is reasonably matched to that of the project's cash flows, we can reduce significantly the interest element of the total project risk. Which either makes it a safer investment, or 'frees up' risk capacity for more productive use.

However, sometimes we must employ special instruments for our interest risk control. These break into two main types:

(i) **forward rate agreements** (FRAs) and **interest rate futures**

(ii) **swaps**.

Both are covered by the term **derivative**, but the word is used rather indiscriminately for any financial construction that is 'synthesised' rather than directly representing a 'traditional' instrument. A derivative is a financial product whose performance is based on the price movement in an underlying asset. The asset might be a bond, share or lump of gold. You can buy or sell a derivative without having to buy or sell the underlying asset. So, while the US Treasury 30-year Bond is not a derivative, the 'long bond' futures contract (which is based on the 30-year) most certainly is. It is advisable to be precise and use terms like 'swap', 'futures', 'FRA', etc. and leave the woolly 'derivatives' descriptor to others, except when you really are referring to the generalised concept rather than to a specific product type.

We will discuss 'swaps' in Section 7. In this section we look at the first group of instruments: forward rate agreements (FRAs) and interest rate futures.

Both are instruments designed to help 'lock in' interest rates, and are close cousins; the key difference between them is that FRAs are **over-the-counter (OTC)** deals offered by particular financial institutions while futures contracts are **exchange-traded**. They are used for similar purposes, the choice between them depending on the particular situation.

'Exchange-traded' means exactly what it says: the contracts can only be traded through the appropriate exchange, and according to its particular rules. 'Over the counter' refers to bilateral deals that are private contracts, typically between a financial institution and a customer. While once such deals may well have been negotiated over a well-polished walnut counter in a marble banking hall, nowadays they are inevitably agreed by telephone, telex or fax. Rather more prosaic but considerably more practical.

As with all OTC versus exchange-traded decisions, the choice is usually to balance convenience against cost. To use a well-worn clothing analogy, the exchange-traded alternative is like 'ready-to-wear' – cheap(ish) but may not fit exactly. The OTC can be customised – tailored, to maintain the analogy – to match requirements, but you pay extra for the privilege.

Hedging means the reduction of financial risk, usually by the use of financial instruments.

6.1 FORWARD RATE AGREEMENTS

A forward rate agreement (FRA) is a covenant between two parties which determines the interest rate that will apply to notional loans or deposits on a predetermined date in the future and for a specified period. It does not necessarily involve either a loan or a deposit, and is simply a formal promise between two parties to compensate each other for the difference between the agreed FRA rate and the relevant market interest rate at the start of the notional transaction.

FRAs are forward contracts on interest rates. In Unit 8 you will come across forward contracts on foreign exchange which are known more simply as 'forwards'.

FRAs are quoted in terms of the contract period. For example, 'three against six months' will refer to a three-month period starting in three months' time.

Example 6.1

The Quancrete company finds that credit extended to a major customer is longer than that obtained from suppliers. In three months' time, the company will need working capital for a further three months. On 12 February, the BB Bank writes an FRA for 'three against six months' (or '3 v. 6') at 8%. Settlement date is 12 May. Compare the following outcomes:

On 12 May, the three-month market rate is 9%

Quancrete borrows at the market rate	9%
BB Bank pays the difference between 9% and 8%	−1%
The actual rate incurred by Quancrete is	**8%**

On 12 May, the three-month market rate is 7%

Quancrete borrows at the market rate	7%
Quancrete pays BB the difference between 7% and 8%	+1%
The actual rate incurred by Quancrete is	**8%**

Essentially, by buying a three against six FRA, Quancrete has agreed upon, or 'locked in', a three-month **forward interest rate** of 8%.

It is important to remember that the FRA does not itself involve the borrowing or lending of money, it is merely a contract for a 'difference payment' between the two parties. In the example, Quancrete actually borrows the required funds from one of its usual sources, but the FRA ensures that the net rate of interest is fixed in advance.

Remember, LIBOR stands for London InterBank Offered Rate, and is the most commonly used euromarket reference rate for short-term and floating-rate long-term debt instruments.

Typically, a rate of interest and a market reference rate, usually LIBOR, are specified in a FRA contract. The buyer of the FRA locks in the fixed rate of interest. The contract is settled by calculating the difference between the agreed rate and LIBOR on the settlement date (i.e. at the start of the notional deposit), and this is multiplied by the agreed principal and the period of the deposit. This amount is then discounted to take into account the fact that any payment will be made at the start of the agreed period rather than at maturity.

$$\frac{(\text{LIBOR at settlement} - \text{Contract rate}) \times n/365 \times \text{Contract amount}}{1 + (\text{LIBOR at settlement} \times n/365)}$$

where n is the number of days in the contract period.

Example 6.2

On 19 July LIBOR stood at 9.19%. Widgets plc made a number of FRA deals with its bank, one of them fixing a three-month LIBOR rate on a £10m notional loan one month later (i.e. from 21 August to 21 November, since deposits are usually arranged on a 'spot', i.e. two-day settlement basis). The agreed fixed rate was 9.30%. On 19 August (for 21 August settlement) three-month LIBOR was 10.25%. So the bank made a single cash payment to Widgets plc which was equivalent to the difference between the agreed FRA rate and the going market rate, discounted by a factor of three months since settlement was made at the beginning of the FRA's notional deposit period.

$$\frac{(0.1025 - 0.093) \times 92/365 \times £10,000,000}{1 + (0.1025 \times 92/365)} = £23,342.15$$

That is, the bank paid Widgets plc £23,342.15. This compensates the company for the extra borrowing costs it incurred over and above 9.3% by using the cash market rate of 10.25% at the actual time of borrowing.

Note that in its actual borrowing, Widgets will pay its normal spread above LIBOR.

The main advantages of FRAs can be summarised as follows:

- Future interest rate exposure can be hedged without commitment to a specific borrowing or deposit.

- Transactions can effectively be reversed at any time to the start of the FRA by taking out an equal and opposite FRA, known as an off-setting position. However, if interest rates have changed since the original FRA was transacted, reversal will result in gain or loss. Also, both contracts remain on the books of the transactors until they mature; in other words, matching FRAs are equal-and-opposite but do not eliminate each other, unlike a pair of opposite futures contracts, as you will see shortly.

- FRAs are usually tailored by banks to meet the specific requirements of companies in terms of both dates and amounts, although generally the period covered is three months or longer.

Exercise 6.1

A company, Wembley Wheels, owns a network of car showrooms. The company always has a new peak borrowing requirement in June, July and August, reflecting the seasonal demand for new cars. In April the base rate was at a relatively low level of 6%. The finance director was concerned that the rate might rise before she needed to seasonally increase her borrowing and wanted to protect Wheels' costs against such an eventuality.

At that time, she was uncertain as to the exact timing and extent of the borrowing. However, her projections showed an average requirement of £1m over the three-month (92-day) period, with a peak borrowing of £2m. She therefore bought a £1m FRA from the bank, fixing three-month LIBOR at 6.40% in two months' time.

What would be the effect if LIBOR were

(i) to increase to 7.5%,

(ii) to fall to 5%?

6.2   FUTURES – INTEREST RATE AND OTHERS

We now look at an alternative method to FRAs of locking in future interest rates – interest rate futures. Before doing so, however, you need to read about futures trading more generally, and the next few pages should be seen as pertinent to Units 8 and 9 as well as this one. Many aspects of futures are the same regardless of whether you are dealing in contracts for bonds, gold or Florida orange juice. We will then look more precisely at interest rate futures, leaving other products to the relevant parts of Units 8 and 9.

BOX 6.1   THE BIRTH OF FUTURES

The first important exchange-traded futures contracts were developed in Chicago in the middle of the nineteenth century. Osaka might dispute this, since merchants there had a form of rice futures contract 250 years ago, but Chicago is normally regarded as the birthplace of modern futures. In the 1840s Chicago became the market centre for grain from the farmlands of Illinois, Michigan, Indiana and Wisconsin. After the harvest, large quantities of grain came to the city in loaded carts, resulting in queues stretching a number of miles.

Unfortunately, there were no adequate storage facilities in the city and, furthermore, the merchants did not have the capital required to buy all the grain that was needed. The result was that only a proportion of the grain could be bought and, often, the farmers who could not sell their product found it more economical to dump it rather than cart it all the way home. In the Autumn there was plenty of bread, but grain ran out in the winter and the price of bread often trebled as new grain had to be carted in. In 1848, the grain merchants formed the Board of Trade of the City of Chicago to create an organised market, and by the early 1870s the elements of a futures market were in place. This incorporated a totally new method of trading, futures, which we shall describe shortly.

The introduction of futures contracts on **financial instruments** is much more recent: in 1971 **foreign currency futures** were introduced, in 1975 **interest rate futures** were started and in 1982 **stock index futures** were launched. Chicago played a key role in all these areas because of its long experience in commodity futures, and it is still the world's major market centre for futures, although a number of new exchanges have now started futures trading, including financial centres such as London, Frankfurt, Singapore and Tokyo. Indeed, the competition between rival exchanges is fierce and drives continuous development of both products and systems, which is to the benefit of customers.

Forwards and futures

Futures trading is a development of a much older practice, that of forward trading, and since forward trading is a simpler concept, we explain it first. A forward trade is a contract between two parties, for one to deliver to the other a specified quantity of goods of a specified quality at a specified date in the future and at an agreed price. No money changes hands at the time and buyers pay the agreed price only when they receive the goods. An FRA is a type of over-the-counter 'forward trade' for short-term interest rate products.

Example 6.3

In the middle of April, farmer Jones agrees to deliver to grain merchant Smith 5,000 bushels of wheat in the first week of October at $3 a bushel.

The advantage of this kind of contract to farmer Jones is that he knows that his wheat is sold, and that he will get a predetermined price even if the price of wheat collapses between April and October. Perhaps his bank manager is more likely to agree to the increase in overdraft he may need to harvest because the bank manager also knows that the money is coming in. The advantage to grain merchant Smith is that she knows how much she has to pay, even if the price of wheat rockets, and can contract to sell it on to a flour mill at a price that ensures an acceptable profit.

Remember Thales and the olive presses from Unit 1!

The kind of forward contract described above has been undertaken for a very long time indeed, and is still being entered into. But, as well as forward contracts, we now have futures contracts. With a forward contract the deal can be for any amount, for settlement at any future date, and the contract is made directly between two counterparties.

With a futures contract the deals are standardised in terms of the size of the contract and the future settlement dates. For interest rate futures contracts the standardised size of one contract is £500,000 on the LIFFE and there are only four settlement dates a year. It is not possible to trade in fractions of contracts. Futures contracts are not made directly with a counterparty, but through a clearing house. Therefore, there is no worry about default of the counterparty, as this risk is borne by the clearing house.

Whether you buy a forward or a futures contract you do not have to hold your contract until the settlement (or expiry) date. If you have bought futures contracts you can close your position at any time by selling the same number.

Conversely, if you have sold futures contracts you can close your position by buying an equivalent number. However, you may lose money if the prices of the futures contracts have changed between you buying or selling futures contracts initially and then closing the position. In fact, very few contracts actually reach delivery. Most (98%) are closed out before settlement.

Example 6.4

In the middle of April, speculator Robinson believes that there is going to be a worse harvest of wheat than expected this year. October wheat futures contracts are trading at $3 and the contract size is 5,000 bushels. Robinson buys 10 contracts believing that the price of wheat (and hence the futures contracts) will rise as October approaches.

(i)   There is a very poor harvest and by the end of September, October wheat futures contracts have risen to $3.25 per bushel, as wheat is in scarce supply.

   If Robinson holds on to the futures until delivery, he will be able to buy $10 \times 5,000 = 50,000$ bushels of wheat at $3.00 per bushel.

   However, Robinson does not actually want the wheat. He wants to take the profit on his trade. So instead he closes out the position by selling 10 October wheat futures contracts for $3.25 per bushel.

   Profit per futures contract $= (3.25 - 3.00) \times 5,000 = \$1,250$

   Profit on 10 futures contracts $= 10 \times 1,250 = \$12,500$

(ii) There is a better harvest than expected and October wheat futures prices have fallen to $2.90 per bushel at the end of September.

   Robinson decides to close out his position to avoid further losses by selling 10 October wheat futures contracts.

   Loss per futures contract $= (2.90 - 3.00) \times 5,000 = \$(500)$

   Loss on 10 futures contracts $= 10 \times (500) = \$(5,000)$

Standardisation makes a liquid market in which people and organisations, who may not wish to actually deliver or receive wheat, can easily and cheaply buy and sell the contract, their reasons for trading ranging from a business need to hedge exposure to wheat prices to the desire for a speculative bet. With a standardised contract, the ordinary investor who has bought 5,000 bushels of wheat for October delivery need not worry that it will be dropped on her front lawn, because all she needs to do to get out of the contract is to sell it before October (this is very different from forward contracts, which may well be unsaleable). Thus, futures have the great advantage of liquidity: the investor can buy or sell them whenever the futures market is open. Another related advantage of futures is that, since there is an active futures market, there is a clear futures price which acts as a signal of the fair market price to all market participants.

The floor of LIFFE (London International Financial Futures Exchange)

As mentioned earlier in this section, the other characteristic which differentiates futures contracts from forward contracts is that, with futures contracts, settlement is guaranteed by a clearing house. With large sums of money at stake, forward contracts may well suffer from the danger of default either from dishonesty or from the straight financial failure of the loser. Suppose, in Example 6.3 above, that in the first week of October the price of wheat has gone up to $3.15. Farmer Jones can then either fulfil his contract to grain merchant Smith to sell for $3 a bushel and get $15,000, or sell on the open market at $15,750. If he fails to do as he promised, the only recourse Smith has is to sue him, with all the delays of court hearings.

BOX 6.2 THE USEFULNESS OF CLEARING HOUSES

The danger of default in forward contracts can be very real: there have been a number of major cases reported, and we shall here describe briefly one of them. The International Tin Council (ITC) was an organisation set up by 22 countries to smooth the fluctuations in the price of tin. In 1985 the price of tin was dropping and the Council backed the price by buying forward on the London Metal Exchange, which at the time did not operate a clearing house. The price of tin continued to fall and eventually the support operation collapsed. The sellers of the forward contracts claimed that the Council owed them £513 million and when the case was tried, the view of the UK court was that ITC sovereign countries could not be obliged in law to pay. Eventually, after five years and several tens of millions of pounds in legal fees, the case was settled out of court with the ITC paying only £182.5m. This kind of risk can be avoided if there is a clearing house, which was one of the innovations of the Chicago futures market and is now almost universal in futures markets.

For many financial markets there are both forward and futures markets available, and which type is used more varies between products. As you will see in Unit 8, in the foreign exchange markets, 'forward' trading volume exceeds that for 'futures' trading, but with interest rate contracts it is futures which dominate products such as the FRAs you read about in the preceding sub-section. To generalise, which form comes to predominate tends to depend on how much extra it costs to achieve the 'bespoke tailoring' possible with OTC products, and how important this facility is for the users. Thus, in foreign exchange, where the incremental cost verges on the negligible and customers often need precise amounts transferred on precise dates, OTC forward exchange deals tend to be preferred. With interest rate products, often the need for precision is less and the extra cost of, say, an FRA is larger, so futures are typically used.

Notwithstanding the point in the preceding paragraph about whether the 'futures' or 'forwards' market is larger *overall*, there may well be a clientele effect, which means that the method less favoured by the whole market is used extensively by a particular type of customer. For example, while overall the FRA market is much smaller in total value than the equivalent futures market, it is very much more popular with corporate users. For them the extra cost is justified by the 'tailoring' of the product. Enough customers must still need or choose to use the 'minority' market or it would rapidly cease to exist, through lack of liquidity.

The clearing house

The principle of the **clearing house** is a simple one: at the end of each trading day each party settles with the clearing house, so as to start the next day with neither a profit nor a loss. Example 6.5 may help to clarify what we mean.

Example 6.5

Suppose that instead of making a forward contract as in Example 6.3, farmer Jones had sold one futures contract for a total of 5,000 bushels of wheat for delivery in the first week of October, and grain merchant Smith had bought a corresponding futures contract. We shall assume, for simplicity, that there are only five days between purchase and delivery. Jones and Smith both open futures accounts, into which they put a cash deposit or margin to ensure that any losses they may incur will be paid. If they make any profits these can be withdrawn as long as the minimum required margin is maintained. In Table 6.1 we chart the deposits and withdrawals in Smith's and Jones' futures accounts as time goes on.

Table 6.1   Margin accounts

Day	1	2	3	4	5	Delivery
Price ($ per bushel)	3.00	2.98	2.96	3.02	3.08	3.15
Smith		Margin account balance ($)				
Initial margin account	500	500	500	500	500	500
Variation margin		−100	−100	+300	+300	+350
New margin account		400	400	800	800	850
Deposit(+)/withdrawal(−)		+100	+100	−300	−300	−350
Jones						
Initial margin account	500	500	500	500	500	500
Variation margin		+100	+100	−300	−300	−350
New margin account		600	600	200	200	150
Deposit(+)/withdrawal(−)		−100	−100	+300	+300	+350

(handwritten annotations: "B", "5000 bushels" next to Price/Smith row; "S" next to Jones Initial margin account)

In Table 6.1, the initial transaction is at $3 a bushel and at that stage both buyer and seller have to deposit an **initial margin** of $500 per bushel futures contract in their accounts. Subsequently on each day, if the closing futures price falls from the previous day's closing price, the buyer's (Smith's) account has to pay the difference to the clearing house, which credits the same amount to the seller (Jones). Thus, at the end of day 2, Smith's account has to pay $100 (= 2¢ × 5,000 bushels) into her account, to bring the balance back to the initial margin. Conversely, if the closing futures price rises, the seller's (Jones') account has to pay the difference to the clearing house, which then credits it to the buyer. This process is known as **marking to market**. The amounts credited or debited to futures accounts each day are called **variation margins**. Notice how the balance at each stage must *at least* equal the initial margin. Surpluses over the initial margin can in theory be withdrawn but in practice may be left to earn interest in the account.

The initial margin and marking to market mechanism is cumbersome, since it involves a daily payment by either the seller or the buyer. However, it has some crucial features:

- It totally separates the two counterparties for each transaction. When the initial trade is done, through a broker or direct with a market maker, the buyer and seller agree on a price without knowing each other's identity. After the deal is done each party deals purely with the clearing house, to whom it pays, or from whom it receives, payment – there is no reason for farmer Jones even to be aware that Smith may have sold the futures to Robinson, as this does not impinge on him at all. In fact the clearing house is not even interested in the chain of transactions: if at delivery time a buyer requests physical delivery, all the clearing house does is to pick a seller from whom it requests delivery. This is an important factor in the marketability of futures.

- At delivery time, both buyer and seller are indifferent as to whether there is physical delivery or not; indeed many may be seriously inconvenienced by physical delivery. If you are a grain merchant, taking delivery of 5,000 bushels of wheat may all be in a day's work, if you are an individual living in a 15th-floor city-centre apartment it may not! This can be illustrated from our example, recalling that at delivery time the futures price must equal the spot price (that is, the price of goods for immediate delivery). Through the marking to market procedure, the buyer's and seller's accounts have been reflecting the *current* futures market price at delivery. At maturity, the futures price is just equal to the spot price so that each side may as well deal on the open market to buy and sell. In other words, grain merchant Smith can afford to pay the current price of $3.15 for the grain she needs for physical delivery. Her *net* price is $3.00 a bushel, made up of a profit of $0.15 a bushel on her futures contract and the current market price of $3.15. She can buy the grain for physical delivery from Jones or anybody else, whoever is most convenient.

The last point made above explains why, in the vast majority of futures contracts, there is no physical delivery at the end. In fact there are a number of futures contracts where physical delivery is not even allowed by the rules, for instance on the eurodollar futures and stock index futures. However, although rare, physical delivery is present as a possibility on many contracts as a means of ensuring that futures prices correspond to spot prices at delivery time.

We have seen the advantages to hedgers and traders of a cleared futures market, but how does the clearing house protect itself from default? The first method is to limit who can deal directly with the clearing house. For example, in London, clearing is done by the London Clearing House (LCH), an independent firm owned by the major UK banks. Certain members of LIFFE are Clearing House members, and the clearing house deals only with these members, whose credit rating has been rigorously checked. Any business transacted through a non-member of the clearing house has to be channelled through a member who may well ask the non-member for additional financial reassurance before allowing them to trade.

In cases of high price volatility the exchange can request 100% of the contract value as initial margin. These situations, however, are very rare.

The second method of protection is the margin system. In order to deal in futures, any investor needs to deposit an initial margin of usually between 1% and 10% of the position taken (in Example 6.5 it was 3.3%). The relatively small size of the margin leads to a very important property of futures: they are a highly geared form of investment. If, for instance, the margin is 5% and the underlying asset only moves up by 2%, then the buyer makes a return on their margin of $2/5 = 40\%$, so that high returns on capital invested can be made (or lost) on futures.

BOX 6.3   HOW MUCH MARGIN?

The margin percentage required varies between products, and is even occasionally changed within a product-type. The general rule is that the margin should represent the maximum daily variation in price expected under 'normal' conditions, i.e. allowing for normal levels of volatility, but not for rare events such as the stock market crashes of 1929 or 1987.

The intention is to give the clearing house enough 'cushion' so that if a trader defaults, the house can then trade in the market to replace the miscreant without suffering a net loss. So on the one hand the limit must be high enough to protect the clearing system but, on the other hand, low enough not to represent a serious discouragement to use of the exchange.

While the examples in B821 will take a fairly simple attitude to calculation of margin based on individual contract holdings, in reality the exchanges use very complex calculations which take into account the overall positions of their account-holders, i.e. a certain amount of netting-off is allowed to reduce the total margin required. This benefit tends to be restricted to the direct members of the clearing system; normal customers dealing through a broker are unlikely to have their own margin calls reduced similarly – unless they are *very* important clients. For most users, since the 'basic' margin amounts are scarcely large to begin with, it is seldom worth trying to reduce them still further.

Since initial and variation margins both serve the purpose of ultimately covering the clearing house against movements in the futures price between successive daily marking to market, the amount of money in either the buyer's or seller's account should never be *less* than the initial margin. As marking to market is done daily, the clearing house should never lose money if a buyer or seller defaults. If, on any day, an investor fails to respond to a call for more funds his account is immediately closed. In the case of the International Tin Council, if the forwards had been marked to market the £528m of losses in 1985 would have been paid over as the situation developed, so that there would have been no necessity to go to court.

Exercise 6.2

In a number of futures markets the maximum movement up and down for each type of contract in a day is prescribed. When the limit is reached the contract is closed for the day, so that no more trading takes place. What, in your view, are the advantages and disadvantages of the setting of such limits?

Short-term interest rate futures

Interest rate futures contracts for short-term three-month loan periods are usually priced on an index basis where the contract price is given as 100 minus the futures interest rate. For example, a three-month interest rate futures contract based on a notional 8% Eurodollar bond would be quoted, not a s 8%, but as (100 − 8.00) = 92.00.

Therefore, if interest rates on three-month Eurodollar bonds rise, say to 9%, the price will fall to (100 − 9.00) = 91.00. If the three-month Eurodollar rate falls to 7%, the price of the futures contract will rise to (100 − 7.00) = 93.00.

See Table 5.1, where the price of bond A falls as the YTM rises.

This preserves the normal inverse relationship between financial asset prices and interest rates. The three-month sterling interest rate contract may be taken as an example. The contract is based on a notional £500,000 three-month deposit and is settled at a price determined by the interest rate at which three-month deposits are being offered to prime banking names in London (i.e. three-month LIBOR).

Currently, LIFFE futures contracts mature once a quarter in March, June, September and December; in certain futures markets, notably the US Eurodollar market, there are three-month futures prices quoted out as far as four years ahead. In the UK, there are at any time eight contract months available for trading, since a new contract for 24 months ahead is introduced as one comes to delivery. However, trading is heavily concentrated in the 'near' – i.e. within 12 months – contracts, and especially in the next contract due for delivery.

The minimum price fluctuation (the 'tick') is one basis point, 1/100 of a percentage point. Since each contract is on a notional £500,000 three-month deposit, the value of each basis point change is:

$$0.01\% \times £500,000 \times ¼ \text{ of one year} = £12.50$$

One tick, £12.50 in this case, is therefore the change in total interest paid for a 0.01% change in the interest rate.

Example 6.6

On 1 February a corporate borrower has a £1m three-month loan from the money market which costs 7% per annum and will be rolled over (i.e. renewed) on 1 May. The borrower wants protection against a rise in interest rates, and considers using two three-month interest rate futures contracts of £500,000 face value each to hedge the £1m loan.

The borrower arranges to sell two June futures contracts (remember a June futures contract is based on a notional three-month deposit beginning in June). The futures contracts are priced by subtracting the implied annualised LIBOR interest rate from 100. Market expectations are such that the implied rate on June futures contracts when sold on 1 February is equal to the present spot rate, i.e. 7%. The price of the futures contracts will therefore be 93.00. In brief, the market expects no change in interest rates between 1 February and the beginning of June.

Now let us assume that, when the loan is rolled over on 1 May, interest rates have risen to 8.5% and implied rates in the futures market have moved similarly. The price of a June futures contract will have fallen to 91.50, that is 100 – 8.50. The borrower buys an offsetting contract at the lower price.

Note that the borrower has to reverse the hedge by buying back two June contracts; if an FRA had been used, it could probably have been arranged to mature on 1 May, the required date. Futures were used because they were cheaper overall.

Since each futures contract has a £500,000 face value, the 1.5% increase in interest rates (150 basis points) results in a gain of:

$$2 \text{ contracts} \times 1.5\% \text{ increase} \times £500,000 \times ¼ \text{ of the year} = £3,750$$

or

$$2 \text{ contracts} \times 150 \text{ basis points (ticks)} \times £12.50 = £3,750$$

When the loan is rolled over on 1 May, the borrower has to pay 8.5% in the cash market, costing $£1,000,000 \times 0.085 \times \frac{1}{4} = £21,250$ for the three month loan; but he has gained £3,750 from the futures hedge, so his net interest cost is £17,500. This equates to a net rate of 7%, as expected and required.

The actual cash flows which take place when you buy or sell futures contracts include the payment of margins. Whether you buy or sell futures contracts, there is an initial margin on opening the position, followed by a daily variation margin as the position is marked to market. You close out your position by buying back a contract you have previously sold, or by selling a contract you have previously bought. In terms of cash flows, your account will be up to date as far as profits or losses are concerned and once the position is closed there will be no more changes in variation margin.

Long-term interest rate futures

Long-term interest rate futures are quoted directly in terms of the buying price, so that a quote of 109 means the buyer pays £109 for £100 nominal of gilt-edged stock. On LIFFE the contract size is £10,000 nominal for the long gilt future, which is the long-term interest rate contract. As with most futures based on long-dated bonds, there are usually a variety of debt issues which fall within the contract specification, but at any particular time there will be one that is '**cheapest to deliver**', and – for obvious reasons – the futures price tracks that particular bond.

So how do we calculate the value of a long-term bond future? A simple **arbitrage** argument sets the value of the futures contract, based on the concept of **cash and carry**. The trader has the choice of:

Method A

Borrow money, buy the bond now, and repay the loan on expiry.

Method B

Buy the futures contract, which involves paying for the bond on expiry of the futures contract.

> An arbitrage is where a *riskless* profit can be made by exploiting different prices for the same product.

Both methods involve no initial outlay but end up with the trader owning the bond; in A she receives the bond immediately but only pays out cash (including accrued interest) on expiry of the loan. In B, the bond is bought and paid for at the expiry of the futures contract, paying the price current at that time; however, any price change for the bond over the period is balanced by an equivalent movement in the futures price, so the net cost is just the price initially contracted for through buying the futures contract. Since the initial and final situations are the same whichever method is chosen, and if we have a loan and a futures contract with the same expiry date, overall A or B should cost the same amount.

If we define:

F = futures price

P = bond price

r_S = the yield of the bond over the time to delivery (in terms of accrued interest)

r_B = the borrowing cost of money over the time to expiry

the cost of method A is $P(1 + r_B - r_S)$, and the cost of method B is just F.

Equating the costs, we get:

$$F = P(1 + r_B - r_S).$$

So, for example, if the price of the bond is £109, the short-term interest rate is 7% p.a., the yield on long gilts is 6% p.a., and the time to delivery of the futures contract is three months, then

$$109 \, (1 + (0.07 - 0.06) \times \text{¼ of the year}) = 109 \, (1 + 0.0025)$$

$$\Rightarrow F = 109.27$$

The cost of carry for non-financial futures would also include cost of storage and insurance. For financial futures the cost of carry is entirely made of interest income.

The difference $r_B - r_S$ is called the '**cost of carry**', to reflect how much it would cost to 'carry' the bond rather than buy the futures. In this case it is 1% per annum, or 0.25% per three months. Notice that with a *positive* cost of carry, as we have here, the futures should be priced *higher* than the bond itself.

Exercise 6.3

If the short-term interest rate in the 'cash and carry' example above had been 4.5%, with all the other numbers unchanged, what would have been the breakeven futures price?

In practice, all participants in the market watch the cash–futures relationship, hoping to find the relationship out of line. If they do, they can either buy under method A and sell under method B or vice versa. This is known as arbitrage. As mentioned on p. 69, it is this possibility of making a risk-free profit which provides the practical mechanism for usually keeping the cash and futures prices aligned, as soon as the two drift apart by more than the dealing costs, arbitrage trades will upset supply and demand until the prices adjust to remove the gains.

Activity 6.1

Using your Web access, have a look at the websites of some of the futures exchanges. You will find links for some of them in the B821 location of the OUBS site.

You should at least have a look at the range of contracts offered by the relevant exchanges; hopefully, you will find other aspects of the sites interesting too. For example, the LIFFE site describes the hand signals used by the traders in pits to indicate how many of what contract at what price they are offering/bidding for. Admittedly a somewhat specialised skill, but the system is based on that used by bookmakers so it may prove useful if you are an aficionado of the 'sport of kings'...

Interest rate futures can be used – and are to a great extent – as speculative rather than hedge instruments, but in this block we are primarily considering corporate risk management, which usually involves risk *reduction* rather than using these products to take on interest risk. Nevertheless, you should always remember that it is the speculators in the market who provide the liquidity which is necessary to allow corporate hedgers to complete their required transactions in a timely way.

UNIT 7 RISK ASSESSMENT AND INTEREST RATE RISK

BOX 6.4 SYNTHETIC PORTFOLIOS

These days it is possible to create a whole investment portfolio based on using futures, etc. for the risk element and which puts the actual cash into very low-risk instruments such as government bonds. The aim is to replicate the risk/return profile of a traditional fund but with lower handling costs.

Given the broad spread of futures and options products now actively traded, a synthetic portfolio can include risk and return linked to instruments ranging from equities to Florida orange juice, with property for added spice.

However, futures and other derivatives can also be used to help optimise more traditional portfolios. An example should demonstrate how.

Let us assume a pension fund has a £50m UK equity portfolio (well diversified, naturally!). The fund manager and the trustees are agreed that the outlook for the UK market is not very attractive for the next six months, at least not in comparison with that for the US stock market. They wish, therefore to shift their exposure to the US for the next six months.

In the past this would have involved four sets of dealing costs, selling UK stocks, buying US stocks now and the reverse in six months' time. Granted, these 'block deals' would attract low levels of commission but still the total charges would be significant.

Instead, they could leave the *cash* investment unchanged, simply shifting the *risk* to US exposure, by trading futures contracts.

To fulfil their requirements, the fund manager would sell £50m equivalent of the London FT-SE futures contract, simultaneously buying the equivalent amount of the US S&P 500 contracts. This operation (and the reversal in six months time) would almost certainly be much cheaper than the cash market trades.

It would also have the benefit of being quicker to execute, and permit 'fine tuning' whenever required, simply by changing the futures holdings.

6.3 WORKED EXAMPLES

Let us conclude this section with a few worked examples. In each case the 'solution' will be given in terms of the products used to hedge the risk, but not the actual prices at which they would be transacted. If you choose to do so, and it would be useful practice if you did, complete the analysis by taking current futures prices at the time of study; these are available either in financial newspapers (e.g. the *Financial Times* or the *Wall Street Journal*) or direct from the exchanges through their web pages, links for which can be found on the B821 site. If you have access to FRA prices, do the same. Unfortunately, at the time of writing such prices are less easy to obtain unless you have a financial markets terminal such as Reuters, Telerate or Bloombergs. It would be worth looking around the Web, however, because more and more information is being made freely available all the time. The free information is usually a minimum of 20 minutes old so as not to undermine the providers marketing to traders and financial institutions, but such data is definitely good enough for this exercise. Indeed, for a generalist manager it will be sufficient for 99% of risk estimation purposes.

We have provided links to some such data sources on the B821 website.

THE OPEN UNIVERSITY BUSINESS SCHOOL **69**

Example 6.7 Short-term hedge

A company knows that it will need to borrow 4.5m euros for three months starting in seven months' time; it is concerned that interest rates for euros could well rise in the interim period, and thus wants to lock in to the current level of rates. For this example let us take 'today's' date as mid-February.

Solution A Using FRAs

The company approaches its bankers and negotiates a '7 v 10' FRA on €4,500,000 where it receives compensation if rates rise above the specified percentage or pays the bank if they fall below it.

Solution B Using futures

The FRA method is simple and straightforward; unfortunately it may also be relatively expensive compared to hedging with futures. If so, what futures contracts could the company take on instead?

Checking LIFFE's website, we can see that they trade a three-month euro interest rate future contract. The contract size is €1,000,000 and prices are quoted on the basis of (100 – interest rate). Delivery is the usual March, June, September, December. The exact day is 'one business day prior to the third Wednesday of the delivery month', in practice roughly the middle of the month.

The hedge is required to protect a future loan from rises in interest rates, so by *selling* the appropriate futures contracts the company can achieve its aim. Note that as interest rates *rise* the price of this euro contract will *fall* (as it is based on 100 – interest rate), so selling it at the current price will enable the company to produce a profit by buying it back more cheaply if rates rise. Of course, if rates fall then the futures hedge will produce a loss, roughly matching the gain from the loan being cheaper; the hedge *locks in* to current rates, forgoing possible savings to forestall possible losses.

The futures contract needs to be in place until the start of the loan, at which point the interest rate at which the company can borrow will be fixed. The company requires three months of protection starting in seven months' time. Seven months from mid-February is mid-September and so we can use September futures.

Turning to the number of contracts required, the company needs to hedge a €4,500,000 loan, but contracts are only available in €1,000,000 'packages', so the company will not get a perfect hedge. They could choose to be a little bit 'over-hedged' by selling five contracts (i.e. €5,000,000 worth) or a little 'under-hedged' by only selling four.

The choice would normally be made according to the view taken of the likely movement in rates. It is possible the company is not convinced that rates will rise and is just being cautious; in such a case, the treasurer may prefer to be under-hedged. On the other hand the opinion may be that rates are *likely* to rise and, given that they wish to hedge the risk, this view may well be prevalent. If so – and let us use this scenario for the example – the choice could well be that they prefer to be over-hedged, so taking out five contracts.

Note that if we were looking at a hedge for €45,000,000 rather than 4,500,000 we could be more accurate when deciding on the number of

The term is '7 v 10' because the loan will start in seven months and will last for three months, giving 7 + 3 = 10 months until the end of the loan.

If the start of the loan did not coincide with a standard settlement date we could use a combination of futures contracts maturing around the date of the loan.

contracts. Clearly, the bigger the hedge required relative to the contract size, the smaller, proportionally, will be any discrepancy.

We can now combine all of this to produce the required hedge. Thus the complete hedge strategy involves a number of steps. These are described below.

Step 1: Now (mid-February)

Sell five September contracts

Step 2: At the beginning of the loan (mid-September)

Buy five September contracts

A perfect hedge?

In mid-February, September futures contracts are sold at 95.00. When the futures contracts are bought back in September the price has moved to 95.75 due to the decrease in expected short-term interest rates from 5% to 4.25%.

Since each contract has a €1,000,000 face value, the 0.75% decrease in interest rates (75 basis points) results in a loss on the futures contracts.

> 5 contracts × 0.75% decrease × €1,000,000 × 1/4 of the year = (€9,375)

This loss on the futures contract will be offset by the saving the company will make by being able to borrow at a lower than expected market interest rate of 4.25%.

Cost of loan:

> €4,500,000 × 4.25% × 1/4 of the year = (€47,812.50)

Overall cost to the company:

> 47,812.50 + 9,375 = (€57,187.50)

In this case the company would have been better off had they not hedged. However, the purpose of hedging is primarily to reduce or eliminate risk, not to speculate on future interest rate movements.

Exercise 6.4

What would the overall cost to the company be if the September futures contracts in the above example had been priced at 96.30 in mid-February and 95.20 in mid-September?

Example 6.8   Long-term hedge

A pension fund has a substantial investment in fixed-rate sterling-denominated bonds, both corporate and government. The investment manager is very concerned that UK interest rates are likely to rise over the next year; this would reduce the value of the bond portfolio, possibly substantially. He wants, therefore, to reduce the fund's interest rate exposure.

This can be achieved by selling the bonds themselves and keeping the money on shorter-term deposit. This will involve considerable dealing costs, particularly as the portfolio will eventually have to be repurchased when the interest rates begin to look more favourable.

So the manager has decided to hedge the risk using futures; futures is the only choice as FRAs are not readily available for so long a maturity.

LIFFE offers a 'long-gilt future', based on UK government fixed-rate debt of between 10 and 15 years maturity. The contract size is (at present) £100,000 nominal value and a notional coupon of 7%. The pricing is the same as for buying the bond in the cash market, so when interest rates rise bond and futures price fall.

The fund's portfolio has a current value of £17.5m with a duration of 8.6 years. How many futures contracts should be used? The manager needs to think about the duration 'change in value' formula, i.e.:

This is the duration formula derived in Section 5.3.

$$\Delta P = -D \times P \times \frac{1}{(1 + r)} \times \Delta r$$

Since what is required is $\Delta P_{\text{portfolio}} = -\Delta P_{\text{futures}}$, he can calculate the number of futures contracts to sell, depending on the duration of the futures contract delivery bond. In fact, there is always a range of bonds that could be delivered in settlement of the long-gilt futures contract, but there will always be a 'cheapest-to-deliver', and it is quite straightforward to discover which it is, and thus to obtain the required duration figure. Let us assume that at the time the 'cheapest-to-deliver' bonds and thus the futures' P duration was 11.4 years.

Thus: $\Delta P_{\text{portfolio}} = -\Delta P_{\text{futures}}$

$$\Rightarrow D_F \times P_F \times \frac{1}{(1 + r)} \times \Delta r = D_p \times P_p \times \frac{1}{(1 + r)} \times \Delta r$$

$$\Rightarrow P_F = (D_p/D_F) \times P_P$$

$$\Rightarrow P_F = \frac{8.6}{11.4} \times 17.5m = 13.2m$$

So, at £100,000 per contract, the investment manager should sell 132 long-gilt contracts. Since he is likely to want to keep the hedge for up to a year he will want quite a long-lived futures contract, but this has to be balanced by the fact that it is the 'near' contracts that are most heavily traded, and thus most liquid – which, in turn, tends to encourage the most competitive price. On balance, he would probably trade for the second nearest contract (i.e. not less than three months, not more than six months to expiry) and keep a watch on the position as time passes.

Lastly, note that the investment manager will also have to watch whether the 'cheapest-to-deliver bond' changes, as this could mean a change in the futures contract duration.

Example 6.9   SoftKing Trust's gap position

Let us return to the SoftKing Trust example from Section 4.2 and see how we would hedge the gaps recorded there. The final gap chart is reproduced as Figure 6.1.

Looking at the gap chart, it is clear that there are various 'steps' in the gaps which will need to be financed (most of these arise from the building of the new clinic, as might have been expected). We ignore the £200,000 payable in two days' time since this will be sorted out 'now' in the cash market rather than through hedging. We assume that the intention is to take out a £2.5m fixed-rate five-year loan in one year's time, i.e. to match the completion of the new facility.

Currency: __£000__   Date: __18.6.99__

	Tod	Tom	Spot	3d	4d	1 wk	2 wk	3 wk	1 mth	2 mth	3 mth	4 mth	5 mth	6 mth	9 mth	1 yr	2 yr	3 yr	4 yr	5 yr	> 5 yr
Opening +	5					15	6			22	7			53	19	47					
Inflow									20		25			25	25	25					
Net +	5					15	6		20	22	32			78	44	72					
Opening –		–7						–10	–17			–45	–21								
Outflow			–200			–85	–5		–35		–500			–1000		–600					
																–440					
Net –		–7	–200			–85	–5	–10	–52		–500	–45	–21	–1000		–1040					
Net	5	–7	–200			–70	1	–10	–32	22	–468	–45	–21	–922	44	–968					
Cum net	5	–2	–202	–202	–202	–272	–271	–281	–313	–291	–759	–804	–825	–1747	–1703	–2671	–2671	–2671	–2671	–2671	–2671

Figure 6.1   SoftKing Trust, all transactions

Thus we aim to hedge the following exposures:

(a) £500,000 from 3 to 6 months

(b) £1,500,000 from 6 to 12 months

and

(c) £2,500,000 for 5 years starting in 1 year's time.

'Today's date' is 18th June 1999, which is just a few days after the June futures' expiry, so it is almost exactly three months until the September expiry, and so on. This is convenient, but by now you know how to adapt these results for other 'start dates'.

There is a LIFFE 3-month interest rate futures contract, size £500,000, price based on 100.00 – interest rate. So to hedge exposure (a) we would *sell* one September 1999 3-month contract.

Similarly, to hedge exposure (b) we would *sell* three December 1999 and three March 2000 3-month contracts.

For exposure (c) we would note that LIFFE also have a 'five-year gilt' future contract, the terms of which are akin to those of the 'long-gilt' contract but based on five-year bonds. Thus, we would do a similar calculation to Example 6.8. Let us assume the duration of the futures contract is 3.8 years. Making reasonable assumptions about the amortisation of the mortgage loan (i.e. the schedule of principal repayments), let us assume it has a duration of 2.9 years.

Thus the value of the futures hedge needs to be $^{2.9}/_{3.8} \times$ £2,500,000, which is £1,908,000. At £100,000 per contract this means we need to *sell* 19 June 2000 contracts. If interest rates rise between 'now' and negotiating the mortgage rate we will pay more for the loan but recoup the difference by buying back the futures contracts more cheaply.

SUMMARY

This section on interest risk products has looked at the main 'derivatives' available for dealing with an organisation's interest rate exposure caused by its surpluses or shortages of funds in various time periods – its 'gaps'.

Forward rate agreements and short-term interest rate futures cater to the same type of hedger (or speculator); the former is an OTC (over-the-counter) product whereas the latter has to be exchange-traded. The crucial difference between the two types is that OTC transactions are flexible, bilateral contracts between two parties but exchange-traded contracts are standardised instruments. The markets for interest futures are, however, much more liquid than for the FRA equivalents; overall transaction costs are also typically much lower. The choice eventually comes down to whether the value placed on flexibility by the customer exceeds the added cost of achieving it.

The section described in some detail the key mechanisms which allow futures exchanges to work effectively: a clearing house and margins. Remember that these systems are used for all types of futures contracts, so when we look at foreign exchange futures in Unit 8 please assume that the core methods of trading and settlement carry over from your reading here.

7 INTEREST RISK MANAGEMENT INSTRUMENTS: SWAPS

The second group of financial derivatives used by corporate treasurers for managing their interest risk is swaps. These are typically sub-divided into single-currency swaps and cross-currency swaps. This terminology is replacing the older names of **interest swaps** and **currency swaps** respectively, because *all* swaps involve 'interest' and at least one 'currency'.

What is a swap? It is an agreement between two parties to pay to each other a stream of cash flows for a set period of time, calculated on a specified basis on a fixed sum of money. A clearer but less precise definition is that the two parties each take out a loan and then agree to pay each other's interest obligations – they 'swap' interest payments. This may appear rather eccentric behaviour, but can in certain circumstances save money for both borrowers. We will discuss how and why shortly.

In fact, the appropriate circumstances occur frequently enough for it to be estimated that between 80% and 90% of Eurobonds are launched as part of a **'bond plus swap' package**. As long as the borrower *ends up* with the correct funds – 'correct' in terms of amount, currency and interest basis – it is seldom concerned about what are the actual terms of the bond launched into the market. We see companies borrowing currencies they have no obvious need for; the swap converts the inappropriate terms into the right ones.

7.1 DEFINING A SWAP

Let us use a couple of examples to clarify our understanding of this instrument.

Single-currency swap

Company A borrows £100m at a fixed rate, although it actually wants to pay interest on a floating rate basis.

Company B also borrows £100m, but on a floating basis – even though it really needs a fixed-rate loan.

They agree, usually through an intermediary such as a bank, that A will pay floating rate interest on £100m to B. In return, B pays to A fixed interest on £100m. This agreement is the **single-currency swap**, as only one currency is involved; since the interest payments are all in the same currency they can be offset, and in practice only a net difference amount will be paid at each relevant date.

Remember that when we look at the numbers, this convoluted procedure will prove to have saved money for both A and B – so the seeming eccentricity *is* worthwhile.

Cross-currency swap

Company A borrows US$100m at a fixed rate, although it actually wants to borrow SFr175m, paying fixed-rate interest. At the time the spot exchange rate was SFr1.75/US$1.

Company B borrows SFr175m at a fixed rate, actually needing fixed-rate US dollars.

As you probably guessed, they 'swap' interest payments. However, because the currencies are now different they also agree to swap principal amounts, so A has Swiss franc funds and B US dollars, as required. The interest payments cannot be netted off, so the actual cash flows are considerably greater than for the single-currency swap. This has implications for the credit line usage, but is not a significant difference between the two forms.

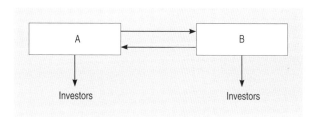

Figure 7.1 The basic flows involved in a swap

A diagram will help clarify the flows (see Figure 7.1). Note that the arrows represent interest payments, and there is intentionally no indication about the currencies involved. The same basic picture works for both single-currency and **cross-currency swaps**.

Remember it is the *horizontal* arrows which represent the swap contract; the payments to investors are included on the assumption that the companies are raising new funds, but it is perfectly possible that either or both of them are managing their debt on a portfolio basis rather than exactly matching each individual borrowing.

This is particularly true if one of the parties – let us say B – is a bank acting as counterparty for a customer. In such a situation, which is actually the typical arrangement, the bank will simply include the cash flows from this deal in its inventory of swaps for trading, in a manner very similar to its management of its foreign exchange 'book'.

BOX 7.1 A SWAP WAREHOUSE – THE ULTIMATE 'CASH-AND-CARRY'?

Although a corporate customer will regard a swap as a unitary package of specified cash flows spread over a number of years, to a bank's swap dealer it is a set of inflows or outflows which can *each be valued separately*. He or she puts each flow into the gap chart at the appropriate point, and bases the pricing of the next swap request on a combination of market prices and what is being held in 'stock' in the 'warehouse'.

Not having to match each deal on a one-to-one basis massively increases the flexibility of swap trading, allowing banks to satisfy client requirements much more effectively. The concept is very simple, but the devil is in the detail and managing a swap warehouse is a highly skilled task (and usually a well-paid one!).

Remember that spot and zero-coupon rates were discussed in Boxes 3.3 and 5.3.

Of course this all depends on being able to value a fixed cash flow at a known date possibly 10 or 15 years in the future. This can be done very easily, provided you have a current list of the appropriate spot or zero-coupon rates.

7.2   HOW CAN SWAPS SAVE MONEY?

A swap contract involves a lot more work than that involved in a straightforward bond or bank loan, so why do borrowers use them? They do so if and only if the net result is a lower cost of funds.

Why can businesses achieve cheaper money simply by swapping interest obligations? Does it not imply that the investors are acting illogically, that the markets cannot be efficient with such an anomaly present? Actually, it is simply a combination of separate and independent investor markets with an instrument which enables the buyer to 'shop around' for the best deal available at the time, across all markets.

There are three major ways for savings to come about:

(i) *Name recognition* – A particular borrower may be more of a 'known quantity' to investors in some markets. Since lack of knowledge equates to risk, the same borrower is likely to achieve better rates (relatively) from investors to whom it is familiar. So if, for example, Redland plc (a UK-based building materials company) needed yen for a Japanese venture, it might well do better borrowing from UK or European investors and swapping into yen, rather than trying to attract Japanese investors.

A related situation can work in reverse, especially for globally famous 'names'. Perhaps Volkswagen Audi (VAG) wants more euros, but the German market is already suffering from an excess of VAG bonds. Bonds from such a well-known borrower may have scarcity value in overseas markets – and so we might see VAG issuing a floating rate bond in NZ dollars!

(ii) *Differential risk spreads* – This is a little more difficult to accept as completely logical, but it is definitely observed to be the case, and the situation has existed for many years.

It is a fact that investors in the fixed-rate market demand a greater increase in credit risk premium as quality falls than investors in the floating-rate market. In other words, floating-rate lenders might accept an increase in 'spread' from, say, 0.25% to 0.75% as sufficient inducement to accept an 'A–' quality borrower rather than an 'AA+' one; fixed rate investors could well demand a differential of 1.00% to 1.20% between 'A–' and 'AA+'.

This is partly understandable in that locking into a long-term fixed rate involves considerably more market risk for an investor than does an equivalent floating-rate deal, but on the whole the difference must be accepted simply as observed characteristics of disparate investor groups. It is certainly true that the investors in fixed and floating instruments form clearly defined and separate sets with surprisingly little overlap.

(iii) *Independent markets* – Probably the largest source of savings comes from the simple fact that the various markets for currencies and fixed/ floating rates are separate and individual, and the interest rates in each are defined by supply and demand in each market *independently*. Different conditions, terms or regulations can apply to, and thus affect, the different markets' rates.

So if there has been a relative shortage of bond issues recently in, say, Norwegian kronor, the supply and demand situation will tend to reduce the interest rates demanded by investors. A 'window of opportunity' may thereby open, making a swap from, say, sterling economic. And we would suddenly see a small spate of kronor bonds issued by sterling borrowers. This would satisfy the Norwegian demand – and that particular window slams shut. And another opens between another pairing of currency and/or basis ...

All these factors are at work simultaneously, and together show why it is that so many public debt issues are done as part of a 'bond plus swap' package. If a company wants, say, to raise floating-rate yen, without a swap, only the yen floating-rate market can be used to raise the funds. The swap mechanism enables the company to look at *all* the markets to see where the best value could be obtained. With so many independent markets available, all governed by their own economic situations, 'weight of numbers' means it is not surprising that more often than not one of the non-local markets offers the best deal. A useful analogy (but do not push the similarity too far) is the difference between a consumer who wants a kilo of oranges being forced to buy from the nearest shop, and being able to get a better deal by accessing the fruit market with many possible suppliers.

7.3   SINGLE-CURRENCY SWAPS: A WORKED EXAMPLE

Let us look at an example of a single-currency swap, to see the flows and savings which occur. Note that in the real market, A and B would deal *completely separately* with the bank acting as intermediary, which would quote to each customer based on its 'swap warehouse'. Nevertheless, it is easier to understand what is going on if we 'recombine' the various transactions – putting together two borrowers was the way swaps were actually transacted in the early days of the product. Think of A and B as 'end-users' and that we have simply removed a lot of technical manipulation in the middle to get to the crux of the matter; in practice A would only 'see' the deal in Figure 7.3 and B would only 'see' Figure 7.4.

Let us assume both companies wish to raise US$80m for five years.

- Company A has the choice of issuing fixed-rate debt at 7.75% or floating-rate debt at LIBOR + 25 basis points (bps).
- Company B, which has a lower credit rating, can issue fixed-rate debt of the same maturity at 8.70% or floating-rate at LIBOR + 37 bps.

This information is summarised in Table 7.1.

Table 7.1 Single-currency swap		
	Fixed rate	**Floating rate**
Company A	7.75%	LIBOR + 0.25%
Company B	8.70%	LIBOR + 0.37%
Difference on risk premiums	0.95%	0.12%
Net differential	0.83%	

The difference in the risk premiums on fixed-rate debt is 95 bps and on floating-rate debt is 12 bps. The differential in the fixed-rate market, as mentioned above, is typically greater, and the net differential (83 bps in this case) provides the motivation for a swap, assuming company A would prefer to issue floating-rate debt and company B would prefer fixed-rate debt but with a lower coupon. Initially, however, company A issues fixed-rate debt at 7.75% and company B issues floating-rate debt at LIBOR + 37 bps, as shown in Figure 7.2.

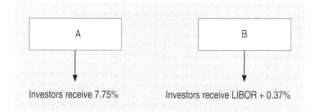

Figure 7.2   Borrowings actually undertaken

Principal amounts: US$80m   Terms: five years, 'bullet' repayment (i.e. all principal repaid in one lump at maturity)

A financial intermediary (a bank in this case) organises the swap between the two companies. Company A, which issued fixed debt at 7.75%, negotiates to pay the bank a floating rate of LIBOR flat (i.e. with no added premium) while the bank agrees to pay Company A a fixed rate of 7.85%. It is market practice in floating/fixed swaps to always pay LIBOR flat, making the rate adjustments to the fixed rate payable; there is no technical reason why this has to be so, it just simplifies matters. See Figure 7.3:

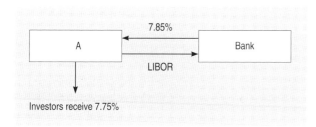

Figure 7.3   The result for A

Company B, having issued floating rate debt at LIBOR + 37 bps, negotiates to pay the bank a fixed rate of 8%, and the bank pays Company B a floating rate of LIBOR, as in Figure 7.4.

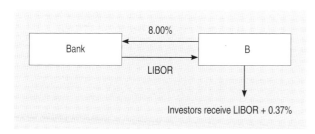

Figure 7.4   The result for B

The total effect is as shown in Figure 7.5.

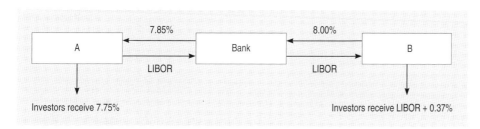

Figure 7.5   The two loans and two swaps

The intermediary bank receives a net benefit of *15 bps*, i.e. 8.00% – 7.85%, the floating side being simply a 'pass through' in terms of rate.

Company A could have issued floating debt at LIBOR + 25 bps and, through the swap, achieved LIBOR – 10 bps. (LIBOR paid to the bank offset by a gain of 7.85% – 7.75% on the fixed rate payments). Company A thus has a net benefit of *35 bps*.

Company B could have issued fixed-rate debt at 8.70% and achieved 8.37%, through paying a fixed rate of 8% and paying a net 37 bps on the floating rate payments. The net benefit to Company B is thus 8.70% – 8.37% or *33 bps*.

The position of each party is summarised in Table 7.2.

Table 7.2 Overall swap gains			
	Company A	**Bank**	**Company B**
Paid to 3rd party investor	(7.75%)		(L + 0.37%)
Bank pays A	7.85%	(7.85%)	
B pays Bank		8.00%	(8.00%)
A pays Bank	(L)	L	
Bank pays B		(L)	L
Net position	(L – 0.10)%	+0.15%	(8.37%)
Cost without swap	L + 0.25%	–	8.70%
Gain	+0.35%	+0.15%	+0.33%

The total benefits add up to *83 basis points*, the net differential indicated earlier. The swap mechanism has enabled both borrowers to optimise their interest costs by accessing the most advantageous 'prices' on offer, rather than just taking that quoted for the interest basis actually required. It has also enabled the intermediary to make a comfortable living!

7.4   CROSS-CURRENCY SWAPS

To complete the review of the basic swap mechanism, let us repeat the foregoing example but assume that A wanted SFr120m fixed-rate instead of the equivalent US$80m. This requires a **cross-currency swap**; note that we are looking at a fixed/fixed swap here, but cross-currency deals can equally well be arranged on a fixed/floating or floating/floating basis.

- Company A wants SFr120m, 5-year fixed. It has the choice of issuing US$ fixed debt at 7.75% or SFr fixed at 2.5%.
- Company B, which has a lower credit rating, can issue US dollar fixed debt of the same maturity at 8.70% or fixed SFr at 2.62%. It requires US$80m for five years.

So A borrows US$80m for five years, paying 7.75%; B borrows SFr120m at 2.62%, also with a five-year term. The spot rate at the time was SFr1.5/US$1.

The intermediary bank does a swap with A, paying the company 7.75% on US$80m and receiving 2.15% on SFr120m. It also exchanges principal amounts for the life of the swap.

Similarly, it does a deal with B, paying the company 2.15% on SFr120m and receiving 7.90% on US$80m, and also exchanging principal amounts.

So the overall situation is as shown in Figure 7.6.

The intermediary bank receives a net benefit of US$ *15 bps*, i.e. 7.90% – 7.75%, the Swiss franc side having been arranged to be a 'pass through'.

Company A could have issued fixed SFr at 2.50% and, through the swap, has achieved 2.15%, a net benefit of *35 bps*.

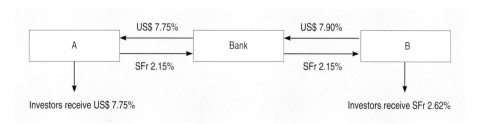

Figure 7.6   Cross-currency swaps, overall position

Company B could have issued fixed US$ at 8.70% and achieved 8.37%, but has a small amount of currency risk because it is paying 7.90% in US dollars and a 'stub' amount of 0.47% in Swiss francs. Nevertheless, it would be likely to go ahead with the deal as the risk (and inconvenience) is small compared to the annual saving of *33 bps* on US$80m. In practice the bank would probably take over the currency risk, reducing slightly the saving offered to B. This is shown in Figure 7.7:

Why 'stub'? Because it is a little bit left over, like the stub of a pencil. Capital markets often refer to any left-over as a 'stub'.

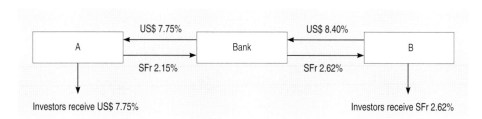

Figure 7.7   Bank absorbing currency risk

For the sake of convenience, the single- and cross-currency swap examples have been created with the same overall saving of 83 basis points. This is purely to demonstrate the process; in reality there is no reason why a US dollar single-currency swap and a dollar/Swiss franc fixed/fixed cross-currency swap should offer the same savings, except by coincidence. Typically, cross-currency swaps offer the better deals, simply because there are so many possible connections between which transactions can be made – there are 15 to 20 currencies regularly seen in debt issuance, each with fixed and floating markets. This provides a huge range of potential cross-currency opportunities.

One can extend the idea of a cross-currency swap into that of a *commodity swap*. The way conceptually to understand this variation is to think of oil, gas, electricity, office rental indices, equity indices, agricultural commodities – in fact almost anything with a clearly definable 'benchmark' price – as new 'currencies'. Just as, say, US$1.70 is the price of £1 in dollar terms, US$15 is the price of a barrel of Brent crude oil. One can define a reference index against which to calculate value changes; this becomes the 'basis' for the commodity swap. The general procedure is now exactly the same as for a cross-currency swap, though

The BBC used to have 'The Multi-Coloured Swap Shop' as part of its Saturday morning children's programmes, but now the bankers can outdo anything offered there, except, perhaps, the deeply dodgy fashion sense of the presenters ...

the technicalities and legal niceties do differ somewhat. Fortunately, for the purposes of B821 you need only understand the basic concept.

The swap market may seem esoteric, even arcane, but it is an integral part of modern debt financing, entwined inextricably with bond markets and other ways of raising money on the world's capital markets. Indeed, swaps are not these days restricted to money-only deals; with 'commodity swaps' you can swap between, say, dollars and oil as easily (almost) as between dollars and pounds. Provided there are reliable benchmarks acceptable to the parties involved, the bankers – and the lawyers! – can construct an appropriate transaction. For B821, all you need to realise is that the underlying principles are the same whatever the constituents, be they dollars, pounds, yen, euros or gold, oil, wheat and real estate rents. Whatever the customer needs, the 'financial engineer' can devise, if the price is right.

SUMMARY

Swaps are an important tool in modern finance, indeed crucial in the field of medium- or long-term debt finance. While not every borrowing for more than, say, US$5m involves a swap, it is fair to say that at the pricing stage of every such deal a swap will have been *considered*, by the financial intermediary if not directly by the borrower or investor. It is important, therefore, for managers to understand the key ideas underlying the technique (as a minimum, so that they can keep an eye on what their financial advisers are suggesting!).

The practical process of undertaking a swap is complicated in legal terms, though the contracts are becoming increasingly standardised, but the *concept* and the basic *pricing* are simplicity itself, the latter really coming to little more than '*x* plus/minus *y* plus/minus *z*' – an arithmetic operation not requiring excessively large amounts of computing power.

Many students may feel that the large amounts talked about in the swap market – for example, the US$5m in the first paragraph of this summary – removes the product from their own level of operations. This is not so, for two reasons. Firstly, while many deals *are* done for amounts measured in millions rather than thousands, this is not inherent in the product. As the market develops, the minimum size for which transactions are done continues to reduce; in particular, as standardisation of the paperwork spreads, reducing transaction costs, the level at which it becomes economically beneficial to undertake a swap continues to fall.

Second, as you will read in Box 7.2, even if your organisation – or you, personally – borrows money in smaller amounts than would justify a swap, the availability of the market to your *lender* significantly broadens the choice of loan-types you can expect to be offered.

Let us conclude our discussion of the swap mechanism with a final boxed example which may serve to bring closer to home this seemingly abstruse element of financial engineering.

BOX 7.2 HOUSE SWAPS

While this whole concept of swaps may seem out of the reach of mere mortals without a £100,000,000 limit American Express Plutonium Card, in fact the method is reaching more of us than we may suspect, particularly in the UK.

It has been traditional for us in Britain to take out floating-rate mortgages from the building societies (the UK version of what are usually called 'savings banks' in continental Europe or 'savings and loans' in the USA) in order to buy our homes. This can cause pain and anguish as interest rates rise, which never seems to be quite equalled by relief when and if they fall again later.

In the USA, the norm is for people to take out fixed-rate home loans, which removes one element of variation from the household budget. But the US savings and loan companies are predominantly funded by short-term deposits on a floating-rate basis, so how do they protect themselves? Up until the 1970s, the answer was they didn't, and when the post-World War Two low inflation, low interest-rate period ended the savings and loans industry rapidly became a disaster area. It has been revived but not without great pain and considerable expenditure of gigabucks.

Also known as a 'billion dollars' – but 'gigabuck' is more expressive!

The UK building societies fund themselves in a similar fashion to their US counterparts, but were more fortunate in that the way the British financial system developed allowed them to pass on the interest risk to their mortgagees in the form of floating-rate loans.

However, in the past few years most of the larger institutions competing for the home mortgage market have begun to offer UK house-buyers the opportunity to take out fixed-rate loans, typically unchanging for an agreed period of two to five years, sometimes longer.

Speaking personally, in early 1997 I had just over five years left on my mortgage, the outlook for interest rates was 'more risk of rise than chance for further falls', and I could not afford a substantial increase in the monthly payments. So I fixed the rate for five years, being willing to pay a bit more at the time for the cash flow security offered.

But the point of this little look into the tawdry finances of a UK academic is: how was I able to get a five-year fixed rate in the first place? Because the building society I borrow from had used sterling single-currency swaps to replace its floating-rate funding with fixed-rate, and thus was able to pass on the benefits to its customers. I, for one, am very appreciative of the fact that there is a swaps market 'out there'.

SUMMARY AND CONCLUSIONS

This Unit has covered a lot of material, and the second half was also quite technical in places. Do not be surprised if your study of it has taken more time than the average for a unit; you may find you need to consider your study-time for this Block in total rather than on a unit basis. Because of the length of the material in the unit itself, we have tried to restrict the amount of associated reading.

As you will be well aware, this Unit can be seen as in two parts. The first part was concerned with clarifying what is meant by 'risk', and with categorising and measuring the risk of an organisation as a whole. This should be taken as informing the complete Block, not just the rest of this Unit.

The idea of risk mapping, or risk audit, is one that is gaining in popularity with organisations as an important tool both for operating managers controlling a part of the enterprise and for senior management when setting overall risk policy. Better information ought to make for better decision-making. Unfortunately, the science of risk measurement is not equally developed for all types of risk. While objective metrics have been designed and investigated for most 'numerical' aspects of business, for example engineering and materials risks involved with production processes, other areas have to be analysed on a more qualitative basis, for example some aspects of marketing. But a risk analysis can and should be equally rigorous whether it is quantitative or qualitative in nature. Management judgement and experience, however, will always be needed when trying to compare results measured in different ways; the analysis is only an *aid* to decision-making, not a substitute for it.

Fortunately, financial risk – which is the key concern for B821 – is one of the risk types that *is* amenable to quantitative measurement.

In the latter part of the unit we considered in some depth the measurement of interest rate risk together with the main financial instruments available for handling it. Regarding measurement, gap analysis and duration were the main techniques discussed. We also looked at FRAs, futures and swaps. Remember that while all three are instruments for dealing with interest rate risk, 'swaps' do so for a rather different aspect than FRA/futures. Swaps are primarily used as part of the capital-raising process to optimise the terms of borrowing, FRA/futures for managing changes in interest rates. Note, also, that 'futures' contracts are available for foreign exchange, equities, commodities, etc., and not just interest rates.

To conclude, a restatement of the aims and objectives of the unit:

By now you should be able to:

- understand the general implications of risk for an organisation, and how financial risk types fit into the overall risk situation
- categorise the forms of risk to which an organisation is subject
- make use of the results of a risk mapping exercise
- understand the concept of interest rate risk
- produce a 'gap chart' for cash and interest risk management purposes

- calculate the 'duration' of a portfolio of cash flows and use the result for quantifying interest rate risk
- understand the concepts behind and basic usage of financial instruments to manage interest rate risk such as forward rate agreements, futures and swaps.

ANSWERS TO EXERCISES

Exercise 3.1

With a coupon rate of 8% and a face value of £100, the coupon will pay £8 interest for each of the next two years. The full £100 will be repaid in year 2.

(i)

	0	1	2
Cash flow	–	8	108
PV @ 8%	–	7.4074	92.5926

Price of bond = £7.4074 + £92.5926 = £100

The price of the bond is the same as its face value, as the yield to maturity is the same as the coupon rate being paid.

(ii)

	0	1	2
Cash flow	–	8	108
PV @ 6%	–	7.5472	96.1196

Price of bond = £7.5472 + £96.1196 = £103.67

The bond is trading above its face value, as the coupon rate of 8% is higher than the yield to maturity of the bond.

(iii)

	0	1	2
Cash flow	–	8	108
PV @ 10%	–	7.2727	89.2562

Price of bond = £7.2727 + £89.2562 = £96.53

The bond is trading below its face value, as the coupon rate of 8% is lower than the yield to maturity of the bond.

Exercise 4.1

See Figure A.1

Currency: £000   Date: 18.6.99

	Tod	Tom	Spot	3d	4d	1 wk	2 wk	3 wk	1 mth	2 mth	3 mth	4 mth	5 mth	6 mth	9 mth	1 yr	2 yr	3 yr	4 yr	5 yr	> 5 yr
Opening +	5					15	6			22	7			53	19	47					
Inflow									20		25			25	25	25					
Net +	5					15	6		20	22	32			78	44	72					
Opening –		–7						–10	–17			–45	–21								
Outflow			–200			–85	–5		–35		–500			–1000		–600					
																–440					
Net –		–7	–200			–85	–5	–10	–52		–500	–45	–21	–1000		–1040					
Net	5	–7	–200			–70	1	–10	–32	22	–468	–45	–21	–922	44	–968					
Cum net	5	–2	–202	–202	–202	–272	–271	–281	–313	–291	–759	–804	–825	–1747	–1703	–2671	–2671	–2671	–2671	–2671	–2671

Figure A.1

Exercise 5.1

(i)

Time (year)	CF £	DF (10%)	PV(CF) £	$t \times$ PV(CF)
1	–	0.9091	–	–
2	–	0.8264	–	–
3	–	0.7513	–	–
4	100	0.6830	68.30	273.20
			68.30	273.20

Duration $= \dfrac{273.20}{68.30} = 4$ years

For a zero-coupon bond the duration is the same as the maturity.

(ii)

Time (year)	CF £	DF (10%)	PV(CF) £	$t \times$ PV(CF)
1	5	0.9091	4.5455	4.5455
2	5	0.8264	4.1320	8.2640
3	5	0.7513	3.7565	11.2695
4	105	0.6830	71.7150	286.8600
			84.1490	310.9390

$$\text{Duration} = \frac{310.9390}{84.1490} = 3.695 \text{ years}$$

For a 5% bond the duration is less than the maturity of the bond.

(iii)	Time (year)	CF £	DF (10%)	PV(CF) £	$t \times$ PV(CF)
	1	20	0.9091	18.182	18.182
	2	20	0.8264	16.528	33.056
	3	20	0.7513	15.026	45.078
	4	120	0.6830	81.960	327.840
				131.696	424.156

$$\text{Duration} = \frac{424.156}{131.696} = 3.22 \text{ years}$$

For a 20% bond the duration is much less than the maturity of the bond.

Exercise 5.2

$$\begin{aligned} \Delta P &= (-D \times P \times \Delta r)/(1 + r) \\ &= (-3 \times 100 \times -0.01)/(1 + 0.10) \\ &= 3/1.1 \\ &= 2.73 \text{ i.e. the price would rise to } £102.73 \end{aligned}$$

Exercise 6.1

(i)   The contract would be settled at:

$$\frac{(0.075 - 0.064) \times \dfrac{92}{365} \times £1,000,000}{\left(1 + \left(0.075 \times \dfrac{92}{365}\right)\right)} = £2,721.16$$

The bank would pay Wembley Wheels £2,721.16 to compensate for the extra borrowing costs of 1.1%.

(ii) The contract would be settled at:

$$\frac{(0.05 - 0.064) \times \dfrac{92}{365} \times £1,000,000}{\left(1 + \left(0.05 \times \dfrac{92}{365}\right)\right)} = £3,484.85$$

Wembley Wheels would pay the bank £3,484.85 to compensate for the fall in rates of 1.4%.

Exercise 6.2

An important advantage of such a procedure is that margins can be set in line with the limits – both the market and the investor can thus be sure that all losses are covered by deposits. Another, and rather more controversial, argument for having limits is that it reduces the size of sudden market movements. Limits, however, lead to the risk that investors either turn to other markets when they feel that the true price is outside the limits or wait for the limits to be revised before starting to trade. There was much discussion as to the value of limits on stock index futures trading after the October 1987 crash. On the New York Stock Exchange, the system has now been amended to allow for a series of short pauses when limits are reached, rather than closing the market for periods as long as a day at a time.

Exercise 6.3

$$F = 109 (1 + (0.045 - 0.06) \times \tfrac{1}{4} \text{ of the year})$$

$$= 109 (1 - 0.00375)$$

$$= 109 \times 0.99625$$

$$F = 108.59$$

which is below the cash bond price.

Exercise 6.4

Profit on futures contracts – The futures were sold for 96.30 and bought back at 95.20.

5 contracts $\times$ 1.10% increase $\times$ €1,000,000 $\times \tfrac{1}{4}$ of the year = €13,750 profit

Cost of loan – A September futures price of 95.20 implies a short-term interest rate of 4.8%.

€4,500,000 $\times$ 4.8% $\times \tfrac{1}{4}$ of the year = €54,000

Overall cost to the company

€54,000 − €13,750 = €40,250

APPENDIX SOUTH EASTERN TELEVISION

This regional TV company has made a pilot programme of a newly devised situation comedy. The pilot programme has been screened in its own region and was well received. The company now has the option of selling the idea and the pilot (for £75,000) to a rival company to develop, or it can decide to develop the pilot into a series itself. In the latter case it is thought the chances of success or failure are equal. If the series were unsuccessful, the idea would be abandoned, having lost the company £50,000. If the first series were successful, another series would be made. Again, it is thought that success or failure of the second series is equally likely. The failure of the second after a successful first would bring the company a total profit of £20,000. The failure of the second series would result in the programme being abandoned.

Table A.1		
Option	**Payoff**	**Probability (%)**
Major success	£3 million	20
Minor success	£0.5 million	50
Flop	–£1.5 million	30

Pay-offs include profits on the first 2 series.

Two successful series would bring the option of making a feature film for the cinema circuit. Three possibilities could arise should a feature film be made. The probabilities and payoffs are shown in Table A.1. Merely continuing the programme for further TV series could be expected to make a total profit of £350,000 including the profits from the first two series.

(a) What should the company do?

(b) If the optimal decision is followed, what is the probability that the company will make a loss?

(c) The decision tree is drawn, the payoffs and probabilities inserted resulting in Figure A.2.

The roll-back procedure starts at node A where the EMV is:

EMV = expected monetary value, a standard term in decision tree methodology.

Node A   EMV $= (0.2 \times 3000) + (0.5 \times 500) + (0.3 \times -1500)$

$= 600 + 250 - 450$

$= 400$

Node B   Rolling back to the decision node B, the choice is between a decision with an EMV of 350 and one with an EMV of 400. The 350 branch (continue with TV series only) is eliminated.

Node C   EMV $= (0.5 \times 400) + (0.5 \times 20)$

$= 200 + 10$

$= 210$

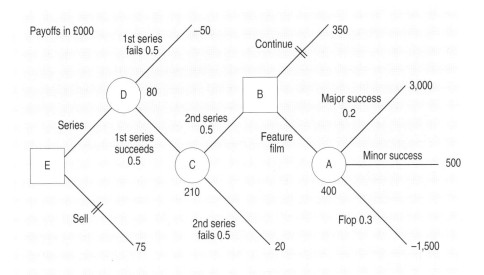

Figure A.2

Node D EMV $= (0.5 \times -50) + (0.5 \times 210)$

$= -25 + 105$

$= 80$

Node E The decision to make the series is preferred to the sell option since its EMV is 80 as against 75.

The route through the tree is:

Make the pilot programme into a series.

If two series succeed, take up the option to make a feature film.

Following this optimal route, the possible final outcomes are shown in Table A.2.

Table A.2			
Outcome	**Payoff**	**Probability**	
1st series fails	−50	0.5	
2nd series fails	20	0.25	(= 0.5 × 0.5)
Film is a major success	3000	0.05	(= 0.5 × 0.5 × 0.2)
Film is a minor success	500	0.125	(= 0.5 × 0.5 × 0.5)
Film is a flop	−1500	0.075	(= 0.5 × 0.5 × 0.3)
		1.000	

The overall probabilities of these outcomes are calculated by multiplying the probabilities of the individual events which make up the final outcome. Alternatively, the outcomes can be viewed in frequency terms (as with expected value). If the company embarked on this decision 100 times, the first series could be expected to fail 50 times. Of these 50, the second series could be expected to fail 25 times (probability $= \frac{1}{2}$). The probability of the outcome 'second series fails' is therefore $25/100 = 0.25$.

Note that the payoff of £350,000 is not possible since that decision branch has been struck off.

Two of the five outcomes involve a loss. Their probabilities are 0.5 and 0.075. The probability of a loss is therefore 0.57 or 57.5%.

In spite of the healthy EMV of £80,000 the company is more likely to make a loss than a profit. Further, one of the possible losses is a very large one (£1.5 million). In view of this, and the fact that the alternative to the EMV of £80,000 is both safe (100% probability) and close to £80,000 (£75,000), the company may wish to ignore the EMV recommendation and sell the pilot programme. This is a further illustration that the EMV optimal decision is a guide only.

Source: Targett (1983)

REFERENCES AND SUGGESTED READING

Eiteman, D.K., Stonehill, A.I. and Moffett, M.H. (1995) *Multinational Business Finance*, 7th edn, Addison-Wesley.

Kedar, B.Z. (1970) 'Arabic Risq, Medieval Latin Risicum', *Studi Medievali*, Centro Italiano Di Studi Sull Alto Medioevo, Spoleto.

Macauley, F.R. (1938) 'Some theoretical problems suggested by the movements of interest rates, bond yields and stock prices in the United States since 1856', New York, National Bureau of Economic Research.

Reddington, F.M. (1952) 'Review of the principles of life', *Journal of the Institute of Actuaries*, Vol. 78, pp. 286–315.

Shapiro, A.C. (1992) *Multinational Financial Management*, 4th edn, Allyn and Bacon.

Swann, D. and Precious, J. (1996) *The Business of Finance: a treasury policy blueprint*, Association of Corporate Treasurers.

Targett, D. (1983) *Coping with Numbers*, Blackwell.

Taylor, F. (1996) *Mastering Derivatives Markets: a step-by-step guide to the products, applications and risks*, FT Management.

ACKNOWLEDGEMENTS

Grateful acknowledgement is made to the following sources for permission to reproduce material in this unit:

Photographs/Cartoons

P.9: © Tony Stone Images; Page 11: Courtesy of the National Lottery; p.35: © Powerstock/ZEFA; p.59: Reprinted with permission from the creators from Stockworth: An American CEO, 1998; p.63: © LIFFE.

Text

Appendix: Targett, D. (1996) *Coping with Numbers*, Blackwell Publishers Ltd.

B821 FINANCIAL STRATEGY